Lin

D1766606

'Every now and again a book co......   ...ges the way you
see the world – clarifying what you have already felt, but never
quite identified, at some intuitive level. This book is one of those.
Read it, absorb it, and you will never be quite the same again.'

Jason Webster, Author of Duende, Sacred Sierra *and 'Max Camara'
detective novels*

'Steve Bonham gives us permission to live the lives we yearn for.
This book is a highly readable manifesto for contemplative action.
Humble, wise, funny and steeped in reality, it is a generous act by a
man who only wishes us a better, more audacious life.'

*Cilian Fennel, Irish TV producer, Storymaker and Communication
Consultant*

'For a psychologist, he seems amazingly sane. But not too sane to
set off on whacky adventures. Steve shows how we all need to
nurture our innate sense curiosity and see what lies round the next
corner.'

Stephen Venables, Mountaineer, Writer and Broadcaster

A Little Nostalgia For Freedom is a timely book. In this age of doubt
and crisis, Steve Bonham leads us towards a more reflective and
rewarding way of looking at our lives, and gives us the tools to find
genuine fulfillment. Laconic, funny and intensely human, I'd
recommend it to anyone getting ready to set out on this journey'

Robert Twigger, Poet, Writer and Explorer and author of Angry White
Pyjamas, Being a Man *and* The Lost Oasis

A Little Nostalgia for Freedom

Living Life to the Full

Steve Bonham

Matador
9 Priory Business Park,
Wistow Road, Kibworth Beauchamp,
Leicestershire. LE8 0RX
Tel: (+44) 116 279 2299
Fax: (+44) 116 279 2277
Email: books@troubador.co.uk
Web: www.troubador.co.uk/matador

ISBN 9781780884158

British Library Cataloguing in Publication Data.
A catalogue record for this book is available from the British Library.

Typeset by Troubador Publishing Ltd, Leicester, UK

Matador is an imprint of Troubador Publishing Ltd

Printed and bound in the UK by TJ International, Padstow, Cornwall

To my parents Terry and Doreen Carter

ACKNOWLEDGEMENTS

Writing *A Little Nostalgia for Freedom* has been an intermittent seven year odyssey. Without the nods, prompts, encouragement and bullying of many people I think I would probably still be writing it. In the early days, Jonathan Glasspool at Bloomsbury and Jo Howard, a very experienced publishing professional, were really encouraging and positive rather than despairing of my unwillingness (aka inability) to categorise this book within a particular genre.

The fact the book takes the style and approach it does – not the way it was originally planned – arose from conversations long, baroque and fascinating, with Robert Twigger and Jason Webster, and a long lunch with Tahir Shah. From these encounters and many beers with my good friend Cilian Fennel TV producer, communications guru and passionate Irishman, came the idea of the 'journey' as a way of exploring an idea. They would probably find it far too pompous to be called 'men of letters' but they live their art and share generously.

Writing *LNFF* in the way that emerged meant that the diaries and notes captured en route became the structure as well as the content of the book. This threw up for me some interesting writing challenges. Making it work would have been impossible without a loyal band of people who read and commented wisely, kindly and insightfully on the several different drafts. So thank you Dinny Eley, Linet Arthur, Jonathan Males and above all my old friend Tim Goodwin whose notes on each chapter ran to hundreds of words. It was Tim too who had lent me the old copy of *Knulp* by Hermann Hesse, that was the impetus for the whole enterprise, as well as a life time of wondering. One day I should return it. If these chapters work I am in their debt, if they don't it's probably because I didn't listen.

Along these years, my colleague and wise and wonderful friend Marie Shelton, has assertively, supportively, challengingly and practically kept me on track. Her tolerance of my tendency to blur work contribution with necessary-to-me explorations of Nostalgic ideas was essential to finishing the book. The fact that it now is will probably be of great relief to her.

This book grew out of stories and conversations with those mentioned so far and so many others including Dave Pegg, Tim Gadsby, David Brech, Nick Owen, Chris and Mike McHugo, Michael Apter, Brahim, Abderrahim Ouardighi, Oliver Barnham, Ben McNutt, Lisa Fenton.

About a year ago faced with a mountain of draft chapters and a bit of a slough of despond about ever finishing the manuscript, Jason put me in touch with Sarah Westcott who bravely became editor. Her positivity, professionalism, sense and sensibility are a major reason for the book being in your hands, as it is today.

Also many thanks to the good, calm and decent people at Troubador who provided exactly the support and opportunity I needed in writing a book that doesn't really fit in anyone else's pigeon-hole.

And finally with love to my family both present and past.

PROLOGUE

The Heaven of Lost Futures

Somewhere in the heaven
Of lost futures
The lives we might have led
Have found their own fulfillment

Derek Mahon, 'Leaves'

I have never believed that it should be 'once upon a time'. For stories, like journeys, never have a single beginning and a single ending. It is twice, thrice, a thousand times upon a time and so it is with this.

In one beginning Knulp lies dying in the snow.

He has been a talented drifter perpetually wandering from town to town, helping a craftsman here, a shop keeper there, ignoring the roving eye of a lusty wife. But now he is failing. He apologises to God for a wasted life, but God comforts him. This was not a wasted life, he promises Knulp, for wherever he went he left a 'little nostalgia for freedom' in everyone he met. For the people he met were good people, steady, conservative but just a little narrow, somewhat unfulfilled, a touch incomplete.

Knulp is a little story written by Herman Hesse. He wrote it in German and this phrase is usually translated as 'a little *homesickness* for freedom'. In fact in all the subsequent editions of the book I have picked up, the translation has been this. But it was the word 'nostalgic' in my edition that struck an impressionable and emotional young mind. It was like an echo of something I'd always felt. It is an enigmatic phrase. In what ways were the solid citizens not free? If nostalgia is a murmur of things that once were and are no longer, what was the freedom they had lost? What might be the things that Knulp's friends had never had, for which they felt regret?

Ever since I read *Knulp*, borrowed from my old friend Tim and shoved into a guitar case as I busked along the shores of the Mediterranean living off packets of dried pea and ham soup, *Vesta* Chicken Supreme and beer, I have been haunted by the phrase and have come to see traces of nostalgia everywhere. I recognised immediately, but inarticulately, the mysterious longing that Knulp evoked in the good burghers – it was a shadowy, powerful emotion that I instinctively understood.

To start somewhere else. Was I was born restless and homesick for another place, time or moment? Perhaps it was as a result of being raised in the sprawling, neat bordered suburban world of Mickleover, a large estate in the county of Derbyshire, where ambition consisted of holding down a good job with Rolls Royce or making railway locomotives. It is just about the furthest distance from the sea in England and suffered in comparison to the birth place of my parents: my mother, a Geordie lass watching the ships sail into the Tyne from all over the world, and my father, collecting the empty anti-aircraft shell cases that fell over Portsmouth as the Luftwaffe tried to destroy the Royal Dockyards. These two great ports are natural begetters of stories, adventures and a restlessness caught in the rhythm of departure and arrival. It is perhaps not surprising that a Derbyshire childhood might seem to lack the seasoning of a little sea salt.

Perhaps the beginning of my personal nostalgia, was an ancestral calling. My maternal grandfather, a tough little man whose personality could barely fit in his 5 foot nothing frame had, before he became a boiler maker with the Swan Hunter Shipbuilding Company, been in the Merchant Navy. My father's family were part of the diaspora of the old British Empire. Great Aunts were missionary nurses in Africa, Great Uncles worked in universities in India, first cousins once removed served in the Royal Navy, others settled in South Africa, New Zealand. More recently, my brother spent fruitless months looking for gold in a rarely visited valley lost in Turkistan, three days mule ride from the road head.

Perhaps it started early. Take Alice. I remember as a young boy, myself, lying in the back garden of our terraced house in Bromley Street, Derby on a summer's day under a lilac tree. Passed on from the upholstered world of the Misses Hays next door, was a colour-illustrated copy of *Alice in Wonderland* a gift from world war one spinsters, who thanks to artillery shells, had no need of children's books.

I read with astonishment the tale of the young girl who leaps down a hole after a talking white rabbit. And after falling, falling, falling she ends up in a disturbingly different world. One in which if you take a drink, you grow small, or if you eat some cake you fill a house with your size. One in which you can swim in your own tears with a mouse.

An exhilarating place, exciting as long as the sunlight from your own garden filters down to show you the way back. But Alice to my horror chose to go deeper. Go back, I mentally cried, get back up the tunnel back into the safety of your own garden. Don't follow the rabbit!

But I understood then the temptation to go further and the trepidation that it caused.

Or perhaps it was the riverbank. I have an early memory, faint with age like an old bleached photograph. So faded I can't be certain it is true, so important to me it has to be true, though I am not sure I can totally trust it. The memory is of standing before the tow path of a canal on a hot sunny day. I am very young and my mother is holding the hands of my brother John and me. It is a present memory.

It is amazingly still, my brother and I have been playing in the grasses along the bank. But now we stand in rapt attention, still tickled by the burr and seed on our bare legs. The air is murmuring with insects. I am entranced. And I am watching two barges move beyond a lock and along water that ran not by a road or a railway line but through the gold of a corn field. From where I stand I can't always see the course of the water so that occasionally it appears as if the barges are floating through the stalks and ears. And most magically of all, I can see that eventually the barges would inevitably and mysteriously disappear into the cool dark of a greenwood.

It was an image that entered into and transformed me, before my mother twitched my reluctant hand away and pulled me onwards. But the image of the little chimneys, the yellow cabins, the tiller held by unmoving men, stayed and haunted me through my dreams and my imagination. And the canal merged into the rivers, and they both ran through the days and years of my growing up, until in my late teens I found the image perfectly drawn by the English songwriter Ralph McTell.

I do remember the times but no number
After the day, but before evening comes
Waiting for castles and kettles with roses
Painted on barges that sailed into the sun.

The image was intoxicating. The canal and the river to a childish imagination was a means to a magical 'next-to' world – a world away from the predictable busy road. For the roads of my childhood weren't dusty and riven with possibilities, they were the functional connection between two suburban points. But rivers meandered not by design but by wilfulness, through secret places, hidden glades; a world gazed upon by jack-in-the-green, the woodwose and the will-o'-the-wisp.

This 'next-to' world, a world of promises given life and image by the flow of the river and canal, and the sense that on a barge you could live on it and within it, became the silken thread of my narrative and my well-being. Time and time again I have been drawn literally and figuratively to the bank of the flowing river or the plodding canal. I have planned great escapes by it, written songs in my head amongst the reeds, fallen in love with the girl who wasn't there, laughed as my clumsy Labrador rolled and tumbled down the muddy bank into its sluggish waters, slipped with it away from the snagging briars of tedium to the realm of possibility.

Somehow, I think the rambling stream entered my veins, and thus it was here that began my nostalgia.

Whatever its beginnings, my nostalgia for freedom has been a kind longing without particular direction, a sense of something beyond definition by cognitive process, a primitive feeling, an emotion without a label, a sense of another world of possibilities. It is momentary, fragile, joyously alive with possibility but also tinged with a melancholic regret for something that cannot be properly grasped or achieved.

For many years this was a quiet and guilty secret perhaps revealed to those with a forensic mind and interest, who might have noticed a somewhat discontinuous career path, an endless pursuit of schemes and other things; and the somewhat distracted air of an outsider.

However, as the years passed, I increasingly began to suspect that this private affliction, like haemorrhoids, undiscussed, might be found in a substantial minority of others. Most obviously, I met more and more Knulp-like characters. People who just couldn't or wouldn't settle down.

She had just come back from a road trip. Having bought an old van on ebay, she had set off with her partner who, if I recall correctly, sports an enormous black beard and manages rock bands destined to remain obscure. Their main principle of navigation was to have no route or plan other than to use conversations with strangers in pubs and with hitchhikers, to strike out in a fresh direction. They slept in the back of the van on blow-up mattresses. They went to little rock festivals in Wales which took place in just two fields, and never got around to seeing what was going on in the second one. They took a suggestion from a friend and went to Laurie Lee's old pub, now run by the son of a famous sculptor, and in a bar full of men who were entrants to the annual beard growing competition, one of them found himself not so alone.

Or my friend Tom: for much of his life he was the personification of restlessness. He had been a right wing public school yahoo, but later joined the British Communist party for a while. He squandered a small inheritance as a would-be racing driver, lived on cornflakes for months writing a novel, sold Rolls Royces in London, and became the token heterosexual receptionist at a very camp hotel in North Wales. Later he settled down, becoming a lecturer in psychology to pre-med nurses in a small college in Yorkshire.

But these were those who wandered. More often people seemed to settle into a well worn path and let the years roll on. I started to see many traces of nostalgia; in places, in people, in the strange and mysterious way we manage ourselves within the confines of our existence.

Listen to the conversation of others. Hear the talk of: the expedition that should have been taken; the love of a lifetime not captured; the friendship that should have been made; the book that was to be written; the exciting job not applied for. Over pints of beer and glasses of wine, late night excursions and the passing dialogue of strangers, flows a litany of intentions and hopes that have slipped like sand through the fingers of life. It is a nostalgia for lives not lived, adventures not taken and possibilities surrendered.

Is it perhaps a yearning not for the basic freedoms of the human existence – freedom from hunger, thirst, poverty and subjugation – but for a freedom which at once can seem more trivial, but at the same time profoundly shaping of experience – freedom to respond to our restlessness.

I wondered why those of us lucky enough not to be hungry, not to be directly oppressed, who have the money and resources to have choices, why are we so often not content?

Are we aware of the potential for that which is new, braver, more challenging, more expansive, that seems at the edges of our awareness, yet too often we fearfully hesitate?

Perhaps we feel we have too much to lose.

And so I began to imagine that, within us all, there is the sense of a ghost of a richer, more passionate, more profound, more exciting, and more complete life.

Later I read José Ortega Y Gasset, the Spanish philosopher. He saw two basic attitudes to life: a healthy view sees life as full of potential to which we are pre-disposed to respond; whereas the alternative view determines that, although such potential may exist, it is necessary to conserve what we have so as not to risk losing that as well.

'An abundance of possibility is a symptom of a thriving life, as utilitarianism, the attitude of confining oneself to the strictly necessary, like the sick man who begrudges every expenditure of energy, discloses weakness and a waning life' and that *'the essence of man is discontent, divine discontent, a sort of love without a beloved'*.

And through the years I also began to see that this discontent may be represented throughout history and in almost every culture. There is a cultural mirror to our inner 'discontent'. For nearly every culture has a place for a next-to world, a magical place, a parallel universe in some respects like our very own but in other ways excitingly, dangerously, provokingly different. Through history and into the phenomena of *The Hobbit* and *Harry Potter* we have created other worlds which both entice and threaten us.

We seem to be hard-wired to fear going there, despite its temptations. The message we hear and tell ourselves seems to be 'don't stray, best stay at home, avoid the arcane and the conjuring of the wizard, the wild horses and the little people. If you go, you can't come back. Be steady, be cautious, dream but don't act, wait till next year, wait till when...'

And so we stay. Put down roots. Get a mortgage, and banish our restlessness to the edge of the night.

But then Knulp comes tapping at our door, we sit him by the fire, ask for a story, a song, let him begin to play and as our feet tap a little, our head nods, and we remember how it was once and how it will ever be.

And the temptation starts to haunt us. To stay or to go? To conform or rebel? To fit in or to fall out?

The more I thought about this restlessness, this nostalgia for freedom, it was a question of how we spend our time.

H. M. Tomlinson was a shipping clerk, a journalist, a war correspondent, a newspaper editor, travel writer and novelist at the start of the twentieth century. Deaf and bald, he always wore the black bowler hat of an East End clerk. The fulcrum of his life was the life and stories of the docklands of London except when, for reasons that are hard to discern in his writings, he boarded a tramp steamer in Swansea to sail across the Atlantic Ocean and up the Amazon river into the heart of the Amazon jungle!

In one of his books, *London River*, he absolutely captures the nostalgic spirit as he watches the ships then moored as far up river as the lifting Tower Bridge:

'A vessel that has hauled into the fairway calls for the Tower Bridge gates to be opened. She is going. We watch the eastern mists take her from us. For we are never so passive and well-disciplined to the

things that compel us but rebellion comes at times – misgiving that there is a world beyond the one we know, regret that we never ventured and made no discovery and that our time has been saved and not spent.'

To save time or to spend it? Now that is the question! In a world in which we expend so much effort on *saving* time – spending time *well* should surely be about being true to ourselves? It would seem to be key to the Art of Life. So why do we hesitate to do the things we really want to do and instead compromise our lives, excusing our dreams as unrealistic or the wilfulness of youth? Restlessness is surely a signal we are not spending time well. Life is lacking something. I have become increasingly convinced that when we say someone is 'shallow' perhaps we should say 'in shallows', for we are talking about a perfectly normal person who has swum from the deep ocean of possibilities to the apparent safety of a barren shore.

Martin Seligman is one of the leading figures in a new movement called Positive Psychology. Traditionally, psychologists and the like since the advent of Freud, have seen their role as making unhappy people less unhappy. Often this is about focusing on our weaknesses. Seligman and his colleagues instead focus how averagely happy people might become happier, building on the strengths that define them. Many positive psychologists also make the distinction between being happy and being fulfilled. In this they are echoing an old Greek distinction between happiness and fulfillment. Happiness is good and even momentarily glorious, but fulfilment (*eudaimonia*) is a deeper more ongoing state to which we might even surrender a little happiness in order to pursue. Researchers have indicated that couples without children tend to report higher levels of happiness than those with children – consider the sleepless nights, the supermarket tantrums, the teenage angst etc. But for so many, seeing their child succeed, flourish and prosper is a reward for all the haunting dreams of infanticide and financial impecunity.

Was a nostalgia for freedom the same as a nostalgia for a more fulfilling life? I didn't know. Both could be said to be prompting us to change.

Now this is the sort of messy thought process that I can work away at endlessly, using the kind of mental gymnastics that on more sober, get-the-job-done days I can put to one side.

But then it did matter – very much. I can't say what prompted this. Was it a phase of the moon, the turning of the tide, a shift in the wind, a cosmic realignment of the planets? The accidental conjunction of circumstance and event? One day, intrigue at a personal and social level became compulsion. I really wanted to understand the suppressed inner adventurer in us. Why the suppression and why the adventurer. And could I say something remotely helpful on the subject?

So began the muddling, discontinuous expedition that was to become my search for the source and deeper nature of nostalgia, and the way that it manifests in our behaviour, culture and customs. The search for the roots of nostalgia, and the way they can be harnessed for a more adventurous life, was a journey of accidents. Its progress was not linear and contiguous. It was a journey taken with less planning than marks the progress of a pinball around the pillars, posts and flippers of the arcade machine.

This book is not a travel journal, nor is it a structured exposition of a psychological argument. It is simply what happens when you go in search of an idea. It is not just the destination itself that leads to discovery but the road or rather roads you take that reveal the hidden treasure.

Looking back on it, the search for nostalgia fell into two parts. The first part was to try to understand a bit about this spirit of who-we-might-be, this core restlessness, this sometimes sense of nearly rather than really being who we want to be. Who is this parallel companion who walks alongside us? It was also to try to understand how and why it arises. Was it just one of the things we all experience to some extent – a kind of mysterious, perhaps God-given bloody-minded refusal to be content? Or are we engaged with some more complex problem that shapes who we are? The more I was drawn into these mysteries, the more I seemed to recognise that nostalgia was an outcome of our essentially paradoxical and irreconcilable nature and our failure to deal with it gracefully. Most of all it arose as a failure to connect with who we were capable of becoming. A failure of nerve.

The second part of the quest was to find out what we could do about it. Through the search I came to the conclusion that there are five 'rules of the road' which, if we follow them, can lead us to a greater sense of being on course to who we might be. And the way to follow these rules is to see life as a continuous set of experiments from which we can learn and evolve.

This journey has convinced me that there is an art to living and thereby feeling fulfilled: it is to be elegantly inconsistent and *let ourselves change*. There is a natural and elemental battle in our heads between the nomad and the settler, the servant and the rebel, the question of 'do I stay or do I go'. It is a constant orchestrator of our experience. It is not just about the literal propensity for wonderlust, but also the potential for a psychological journey through which different perspectives and aspects of us can emerge. Our tribes, our societies, in order to replicate themselves need most of us to be consistent much of the time. Belonging to a tribe is about doing the expected thing, but this may make us feel on occasions like a plug being squeezed into the wrong-shaped hole. We are not so 'resolvable' that we can remain so static.

I believe too that it should not be the seeming hypocrisy of appearing inconsistent that we should be afraid of, as much as the equivocation and 'voluntary slavery' that most often arises from a desperate desire to appear consistent. Audacity, the wilful venturing to the dangerous edge of possibility, is open to us all and through it we can discover first, acceptance of our paradoxical essence, and then a stronger narrative for ourselves that overcomes procrastination and sets us free.

PART ONE

CHAPTER ONE

In Search Of Knulp

Or must I be content with discontent
As Larks and Swallows are perhaps with wings?
And shall I ask at the day's end once more
What beauty is , and what I can have meant
By happiness?

Edward Thomas, 'Glory'

And so began my search for the source and meaning of our nostalgia for freedom. In the brutally honest words of my chum Nick Owen: 'Bloody hell, Steve. You're looking for the *intangible*. That which cannot be defined yet which most assuredly exists!'

I could see he had a point. In fact, it was worse than that, not only was I searching for the intangible, but the whole thing had been provoked by a *fictitious* character. How should I start?

Somewhere in the junk of old notebooks, photos of drunken revelry and long forgotten bills and receipts I located the battered, soup-stained, but still intact copy of *Knulp* from all those years ago.

On one long afternoon I reread it.
Sitting in my Mother's old 'outdoor' chair.
Under the apple tree.

Who is Knulp? Within the now yellow pages, he still walks through the forested hills of Baden-Württemberg in South Germany. Amongst little towns nestled in polite seclusion, two sides of an arched stone bridge under which sometimes disturbingly vigorous waters, flow. Shoes down at heel but clean, clothes a little threadbare but neat and carefully repaired; his hat, like his figure, trim and normally jaunty, Knulp spends his years from early adulthood till his end, on the road, navigating by whim and happenstance.

He sometimes sleeps out in the open, or in a hay barn, but many times is invited in by friends who live in steeply gabled houses in narrow cobbled streets.

To these friends, Knulp is an enigma. Blessed with intelligence, creativity and a graceful humanity, he seems to disregard such gifts and although he does little that is expressly prohibited he carries on 'the illegal and disdained existence of a tramp'. He wants nothing out of life but to look on. His friend, the tanner, 'could not have said whether this was too much or too little.' In the three short episodes of his life that make up the book, Knulp is met with great kindness and affection, but the tanner, the tailor, the stone-breaker, and Doctor Machold, who attempts to look after him in his final illness, all chide him over his wasted life. They are troubled, perhaps they are challenged, by his refusal to seek achievement, position and even take a role within the community of which he is so clearly fond. Knulp, at times, wonders too at the seeming pointlessness of his existence, and he rates his talents less highly, seeing himself as pretty good at whistling, having an ability to play the accordion, an author of an occasional playful poem, and quite good at dancing. He seeks nothing more than to provide a moment of laughter or forgetfulness in the people he meets. Of course this cannot satisfy his friends as they mourn and chide his wasted years.

But why is it that they and we feel such a need to insist that someone must achieve, conform, accept responsibility and 'play the game'? And more than that. Why is that in all of them, he prompts another more elusive reaction, an acknowledgement of the spirit of Knulp's existence that challenges their own decisions about life? For many of them there is a sense of underlying frustration: the stone-breaker wanted to work on the railway, the tailor, despite his early skill and ambition, is impoverished through having too many children too quickly and the tanner has married a woman who will probably betray him. Somewhere at the edge of awareness, perhaps they too wonder at a life they could have led and raise a silent cheer to a dream pursued by proxy.

Why does this happen, how is Knulp so provoking? Is it just that he simply reminds us of our disappointment in a life a little less full than it might be, or is something more profound going on? Why does he, over some of us at least, have this power? For the dream is a constant one. Knulp is an ageless theme in our childhood experience. A millennium of enticement from the clown, the lion tamer, and the sword-swallower to run away and join the circus, the pied piper leading children to a mysterious cave.

And for a while in the daze of the sun, I put the book down and thought about the Knulps of my childhood. There were a few I decided. The ones you were thrilled to see and quietly mourned when they left.

My most powerful memory of all was the arrival, at irregular intervals, of an old friend of my father's. He looked different to the other men my father knew who were well-scrubbed and jolly. When he came into the house, invariably he was wearing desert boots and an old safari jacket, with a thin trail of blue Gauloise cigarette smoke lingering around his head. He and Dad had at one time worked together as surveyors and had become friends, but their lives had taken very different courses. My father's to a small provincial English town, he to take short term contracts in far off places to fund overland photography trips, the magic dust from his boots resulting in an evening slide show which my brother and I were allowed to stay up and see. I can recall the excitement of the screen going up; the dog banished from the room; the buzz of the projector; the familiar smell created as the bulb heated up the dust; then the succession of images: mountain passes, strange looking people, mysterious dwellings and blistering heat. The shame is I can remember little of the detail of the where and when of these adventures, just the mystery and the final disappointment of it being deemed too late to stay up for the next box of slides. And in the morning he would be gone, a man from another world...

The more I thought about it, the more it seemed that Knulp was some sort of go-between from the mundane to the magical. Between the ordinary world in which we so often find ourselves and the way we dream that our world might be. Between the world that we choose and the one we do not. As though he represents a state of 'part-belonging', with one foot in the ordinary world, and one in another.

Lost in the trance of this old book and the afternoon perhaps, I felt I recognised this sense of semi-detachment, of being half in the world and half out of it.

And I thought I heard Knulp say, 'This is how it is when you see the world is not as fixed as you like to think it is, as you feel you are expected to see it. Then you realise that what you experience is made up of the choices you have and have not made.'

But your choices Knulp, I thought, they are not realistic for most of us. Most of us would not enjoy a life on our own, a life that was so uncertain. What we have may not be exciting but it is dependable. Not many of us want to be penniless and lonely.

'Ah,' replied Knulp. 'But there is an outsider in us all, an instinct to leave the tribe, the village, to embrace a beautiful loneliness.'

'But Knulp,' I protested. 'We can't all be vagabonds and adventurers?'

'That is true,' said Knulp kindly. 'That is true. And my friends were good and worthy people whom I envied more than just a little. But there is a difference you know. Perhaps we should not all be adventurers, but there is a little bit of adventurousness in all of us, an aliveness to the unfolding possibilities of the moment.'

'And that is why you made them nostalgic?'

'Yes,' murmured Knulp thoughtfully, as my neighbours on one

side started up a lawnmower, and the old lady on the other side of the fence raised a gin-and-tonic-toast to the ducks she kept in a chicken wire run at the bottom of the garden. 'I did no more than help people see their everyday, just for a moment, look odd and incomplete.'

'And another world more reasonable?'

'We have always imagined other worlds through which to see and judge our own. You called them next-to worlds.'

'So how does this work?' I wondered. 'How do we respond to the adventurousness without taking the path of the vagabond?'

'That was something I never understood,' admitted Knulp. 'I could not settle down, but I felt the loss of it. It was a dilemma,' he said, I thought a little sadly. 'Why did I make people nostalgic, for what purpose?

'Before I finally fell asleep in the snow, I used to have a recurring dream in which I go back to the old town in which I was born. It gave me the weird sensation of things being both familiar and unfamiliar at the same time. The gabled houses are somehow higher, elongated and distorted. People I meet I recognise but they don't recognise me. When I eventually find myself in my old street, outside my dear old house, unnaturally tall but looking familiar, in the doorway stands my former lover Henriette: except she is taller, and somehow different from before and still more beautiful.

'And I call her name, but she is no longer Henriette but Lisabeth, my second great love, who looks at me in a way that is clear and calm, yet so spiritual and lofty that I feel like a dog.

'She turns back into the house and in an instant the town loses its surreal quality and resumes a more familiar aspect. People recognise me once more, smile a greeting, but now it is I who cannot respond. The dream is no different to the bigger pattern of my life.'

For the first time, I thought about Knulp with pity. He could not be absorbed into the world of his friends. In the end, he chooses to die alone in the woods around his home town rather than the sanatorium his doctor friend has arranged for him.

I felt sorry for him as I remembered his 'road book', his totally fictitious account of his work as a journeyman through which he could prove to the police that he was a regular working man.

As Knulp faded back into the yellowing pages of the old paperback book, I thought about the dilemma he left. If a little bit of adventurousness exists in all of us…

Instinctively I felt that this was not just about doing dangerous things, or taking part in wild expeditions, it was about who we are. Knulp's friends represented the cautious and conforming in us, the tribe member. Knulp the rule breaker, the onlooker and the outsider. Knulp makes us nostalgic because the choices we often make relegate this part of us to the peripheries, leaving us sometimes feeling restless and unfulfilled. To deny our restlessness is to deny a bit of who we are.

And lying in the long slow hours of a warm English afternoon, I wondered at the purpose of our restlessness, in our human story, what is it for? And how does it shape us?

The questions in a strange way were deeply and immediately important, but Nick's challenge had not lost its bite: how do I search for the intangible? Was it a matter of studying the works of seers, sages and academics? This felt pretty unpalatable. But then I had an idea.

Isn't it often the case, I thought, that we find something when we are not directly looking for it? We spend all day looking for a key and find it next day looking for something else. Usually in a place we know we examined many times the previous day. I once found my car keys in the fridge.

Sometimes discovering the answer to difficulties and challenges is not always about rushing around looking but standing in the right place so that the answer comes to you. Often the harder you look, the harder it is to see.

I was going to have to search by sideways means, catching things out of the corner of my eye. Or to use my favourite word, to trust in serendipity, the magic of finding things whilst you look for something else.

And it came to me: exploring this idea could be done in the same way that you explore a place. You can string along the tourist trail. You can want to visit the big places with crowds and the glory and the people selling souvenirs. But you might also want to wander off the mainstrip, take the back alleys to the out of the way places where grubby kids stare at you and you find a mad woman whirling about in a jumble of scarves. There you can come across things, half-forgotten, ill-remembered, which make you look at the whole again and notice.

If a nostalgia for freedom shapes our experience, then places must in some way contain it, echo it, be haunted by it. Rather than piling through books, articles and web pages, trying to discover this connection in other people's perspectives and ideas, I would put myself in position where I could see, without looking. This would mean getting my boots on.

It is at the crossroads of place and people, and the accidental meetings they offer, that we can discover the secrets of ourselves. And real places shape psychological spaces; places like the greenwood, the desert, and the harbour. The next-to worlds I had sensed in my childhood, could be the mirrors of internal, mental landscapes. Go to the places, I reasoned, in which next-to worlds were a hair's breadth away from our own, and I would start to understand a bit more about our nostalgia for freedom.

Now, one of the pleasing peculiarities of my own existence is that it is fairly peripatetic, for I live the life of a second rate Medieval scholar wandering about relying on the patronage of local Dukes, Earls and other potentates swapping a bit of insight and experience for a crust and a bed. Except the potentates these days are the large corporations of global commerce.

At the start of any one year I can have no idea where I might end up and in each unanticipated place there is often the opportunity to explore the odd tributary. If nostalgia is the result of an unfulfilling life related in some way to the idea of a journey not taken, then the serendipity of the road should surely offer some clues.

And Knulp could be my guide and travelling companion.

'That could prove difficult,' murmured Knulp, back in the garden again. 'I am long gone, buried under autobahns on which thundering Mercedes saloons cover distances in a couple of hours over which I would take days!'

'This is true,' I thought aloud. 'But in this matter, you are the symbol and the shaman who conjures up restlessness and the magic of possibility.'

'So,' said Knulp supportively. 'Direction was never my strong suit. Who might help? When you were small, who made you nostalgic? Who did you think was adventurous?'

I closed my eyes and let the names and faces from the past rise through the mists of boyhood memory: Robin Hood, Rob Roy, Keith Richards, Top Cat, Francis Drake, Gandalf, Ernest Shackleton and Wing Commander Stanford Tuck!

'Brave, adventurous men who did dangerous things,' conceded Knulp. 'But did they make you feel nostalgic? Are you not searching for the roots of our restlessness? Who made you restless, who called you to something else? Who are they? Who am I?' he insisted.

'Well Knulp,' I mused. 'You are a wanderer, you sing songs and dance a bit, you are bit of a rogue.'

'Start there then.'

People became images. It was Peter Green playing the most wonderfully melancholic guitar on 'I loved another woman'; it was the Texas oilman in the film *Local Hero*, tipping out the sea shells collected from the west coast of Scotland onto the kitchen table of his hi-tech Dallas apartment, and it was the cartoon characters, two dimensional heroes and Saturday morning idols who risked all for freedom, fortune or the buzz of the fool's escapade. It was the spy deep inside the enemy's enclave, it was the lost airmen finding Shangri La.

It was the audacious ones who stood true to themselves and could defy the times, who danced to their own drumbeat, the rule breaker and the rule maker; it was Lawrence of Arabia crossing the desert in billowing white robes; it was Jimi Hendrix's guitar flaming in the twilight; it was the few against the many.

And suddenly there they were: the wanderer-seeker searching for adventure, discovery and enlightenment on the road; the strolling-player whose survival and journey intertwine in the tinker's trade, the travelling show or the sale of camels; and beyond the safety of conformity – the outlaw, also recognised as the rebel, the maverick and the pirate.

'Well there you are!' chirruped Knulp.

'I see the wanderer, and even the strolling player in you Knulp,' I said. 'But you were no pirate. For a start you lived a long way from the sea.'

'You are being much too literal,' he admonished. 'There is a pirate in all of us. Every time we feel outside of the law or not bound by convention, we open up hostilities with the majority. The road was my rolling sea and my passage to freedom.'

'But you didn't steal things,' I pressed.

'Is that really the most important thing about being a pirate?'

And over a while I wondered about these three shadows of Knulp; they all have an essence of romantic mystique, which seems to wrap around themselves despite the often harsh reality of their existence. Thus the lady of the castle runs off with the raggle-taggle gypsy in the folk song; Jack Kerouac, living on the road, is worshipped by Yankee students in law schools and medical colleges; Granddad dreams of a Harley Davison and the delicious Keira Knightley swoons in the arms of a poor pirate.

All three had a necessarily ambivalent relationship with the fixed world around them. Knulp-like, they are 'part-belongers', depending upon the very thing they have rejected. The wanderer-seeker relying on the charity of others on the path to enlightenment and his compatriot, the explorer sucking up to sponsors since before Christopher Columbus batted his eyelashes at Queen Isabella; the strolling player needing the crowd to play or sell to; and the outlaw the rich to steal from whether or not he or she gives the proceeds to the poor.

Like Knulp, they frequently face disapproval from the status quo, in fact in the case of the outlaw and the strolling player, they can be the subjects of outright hostility – even while remaining the objects of Romantic affection. The wanderer-seeker? Even in the personification of the noble explorer we quietly wait for him or her to get a proper job and settle down.

But don't we just love them as well? For they represent something of us. Don't we fancy a touch of piratical swagger might suit us now and again? Wouldn't a life on the road be some sort of salvation even if we reduce it to a caravan holiday down a narrow road? Secretly, don't we wish to emulate now and again, the rule breaking, convention defying adventures of Indiana Jones? These are 'avatars', romantic alter-egos that echo and resonate with our internal debate between the life we have and the life we could have.

I would start my exploration by walking in the footsteps of precisely these kinds of characters, to see the world though their eyes. And then it seemed obvious my crossroads would be North Africa or rather Morocco – the land of the Maghreb. Morocco had to be the fulcrum for exploring a little nostalgia for freedom for it is the land of travellers and strolling players, home to parallel worlds, story tellers and great wanderers like Ibn Battuta, who in the 15th Century travelled for thirty years and 70,000 miles. Even today there is the whiff of the exotic and mysterious about the place. The sunset lands. A snaky line between a desert walled-out by mountains and the edge of the Western Ocean. A land from which the scent of cumin, mint, camel dung and wood smoke is born on a desert wind drifting upwards into northern Europe to tickle the nostrils with a little nostalgia.

And it turns out it is also the land of a nostalgic archetype: pirates. For a conversation with my friend, the writer Robert Twigger, had led to me discovering the writings of the anarchist writer Hakim Bey and his book – *Pirate Utopias*. Hakim Bey, also known as Peter Lambourn Wilson, writes with Ranterish zeal about a moment in Moroccan history when a long tradition and successful history of Piracy consolidates itself into not one, but three Pirate Republics in the late 17th Century including and centred around Sale – next door to the present day capital Rabat. To my mind it seemed obvious that the search to know the freedoms for which, well-fed and secure, we nostalgically mourn, could start here.

CHAPTER TWO

The Light Under the Bolted Door

A travelling man learns all sorts of things
Hermann Hesse, Knulp

I travel chaotically. The secrets of the competent wanderer are lost on me. Considering the farrago of misunderstood directions, impossible connections and incipient disaster I bring to the endeavour, then the fact that I invariably get to my destination is most often due to the kindness of strangers than navigational talent. I learned years ago to appreciate the mystery and the challenge of utterances easily made by seasoned travellers. The sort who, wearing their RM Williams boots, lean back on a wooden chair in the bar, and tell a rapt audience of one 'I caught a motorised canoe and travelled 250 kilometres upstream into Northern Borneo'. Such statements are riven with assumptions and enigma. Why did you go upstream? How did the presumably monoglot native understand that you wanted to go upstream? How did you know where to get off? How did you know how much to pay? Do you tip? What were the arrangements for getting back?

It is not that this has always inhibited my journeys; for some reason the realisation that a journey entails an eye for detail that eludes me, doesn't sink in until after I have taken the irrevocable first step. As a twenty-year-old, I found myself travelling for three days on a Greyhound bus across America in a state of increasing gloom as I had $50 dollars in my pocket, no ticket home and was heading west, a direction that was increasing the problem with each and every hour.

14

I was not surprised, therefore, when I found that the journey in search of the roots of nostalgia began, as with all my expeditions, in a jumble of hasty arrangements and the fog of uncertainty.

I left England at 3.15 am to take two flights and a train journey heading south towards Sale. I sat folded like an old sardine on a plane for Spain, a cheap flight to Madrid, to be followed by a several hour wait and then another sardine-tin journey to Rabat in Morocco – Rabat being the nearest landing strip to my destination.

In the terminal experience of early morning check-in and boarding, I became grimly aware of my complete ignorance concerning how I was to get from Mohammed V airport in Casablanca where my ticket landed me, to my destination on the river Bou Ragreb down near Rabat sixty miles away. I had no map, no directions, no 'how to find us' instructions. Knulp, I ruefully pondered, seemed to know his way around the hills and towns with fluency and direction – or was it is simply he relied on his feet, not cattle planes and public transport.

No one can think straight at an early hour, so I closed my eyes, making a mental note to deal with the problem later. I returned to it in the steamy heat of Madrid airport, opening the *Lonely Planet Guide to Morocco*. At the last minute, I had thrown it into the old leather bag that serves as a rucksack, when I had packed the previous night. The admirable publication was, as usual, tantalisingly unhelpful. What I need is a simple 'get on this at X time and get off at Y and it will be right in front of you'. Instead I read about complex options involving trains and buses and two sorts of taxi. I reread the page several times before coming to the conclusion, again delaying the moment of truth, that the best strategy was to wait and see what happened when I got there.

Instead, I pondered what I was here to find. Perhaps it was in the 'crime scenes' of psychological history that I would spot some clues. I remembered an old spooky television play from the 1970's, *The Stone Tapes*, in which the death of a Victorian maid, and ultimately something much more malevolent, is recorded into fabric and the stones of an old building. An interesting conceit exploring the idea that acts of extreme violence or passion must in some way embed themselves in a recoverable way in the stones.

Less dramatically perhaps, somewhere like the city of London is shaped by the character and occupations of the generations who have lived there since the earliest of times. Would there be hints and traces of nostalgia in the walls of Sale?

Casablanca's airport must be the most disappointing on the planet. It's not the airport's fault per se, but *that* film imbues it with so much broken-hearted mystery, that the absence of Peter Laurie disappearing into the crowd and the chilly beauty of Ingrid Bergman waving hello (or is it goodbye?) always comes as surprise. In fact, Casablanca is just another North African airport, chaotic with a tumult of languages and characters locked in the urgent and despairing common purpose of finding out where to go and failing to line up next.

Feeling a little chastened by my lack of preparation, I found the railway station by a process of elimination, sign language and execrable French and boarded a train bound for somewhere but at least it seemed to be heading south.

As the flat coastal plain, dotted with the occasional rusting junk, dilapidated dwellings and olive groves slipped past the train window and I sipped on a shockingly strong cup of coffee, I considered what I had read about my destination and what I wanted to discover. As the ancestral home of the 'Sally Rovers', the roving pirates of folk memory and folk song, I hoped to find their ghosts in the streets where they trod, and in their descendants, a little of the essence of them.

If Knulp's freedom had involved him living outside of society, then pirates – or at least, so it would seem – lived in a kind of self-imposed exile. Deemed illegal, and ferociously hunted by admirals and generals from before Julius Caesar and onwards to the present day, they set themselves outside recognised rules of behaviour.

But then again, as someone said, one man's freedom fighter is another man's terrorist. Pirates, officially called privateers, in the time of Good Queen Bess, as well as the pirates of the Barbary Coast, were state sanctioned, approved, almost civil servants. So what could they show us about our nostalgia for freedom?

I read recently that pollsters recognise that most people regard themselves as in some sense 'outsiders'. And that they tend to admire those politicians who show maverick tendencies, who are willing to reject the 'party line'. They appear to us as more 'authentic'.

England is not so 'class-bound' I mused since its heroes from Boudicca, Robin Hood, to Nelson, John Lennon and beyond, undermined the rule makers, the bureaucrats, and our self-appointed betters.

I stared out of the window. A mule was tethered to an old tractor. A mudwalled hut with a corrugated roof sat in the corner of a deserted field. Hakim Bey mentioned one particular group within the overall pirate horde which seemed to capture the essence of what I was searching for: the elusive Renegados.

Thousands of Christian individuals chose not only to join the pirates and become Renegados, but also to convert to Islam. It was a huge step. It was to be reviled as scum in your own society. It was forever to abandon the world into which you had been born, to accept that you would be slain on sight in most European countries, and burned to death in Spain. Of course many were people captured by corsairs and turned pirate and Muslim because the alternative was slavery or ransom. Many, but not all, and perhaps not even the majority. What was it that attracted these people to such a drastic choice? Was it, as 'civilised' Europeans believed, that they were simply responding to base desires such as lust, greed and wantonness or was something more subtle and profound going on? Muslims, captured by Christians, tended *not* to convert.

Unfortunately, despite the numbers, little in the way of a

written record survives. Most of the Renegados would have been illiterate and Christian and Muslim historians have, presumably for very different reasons, ignored them. But they must have been strong characters, committed to what they were doing, to take such a step that would be life-changing and irrevocable.

One or two characters have made it through the murky fog of history. One of my favourites is Captain John Ward. A washed up old sailor in his fifties, he was living out his days in penury in Plymouth, when he had the extreme misfortune to be pressed back into service to suffer as a forced conscript in the Royal Navy.

However, old John was made of some stuff. After just two weeks in the Navy he had had enough. Recruiting thirty followers, he captured a small boat and embarked on a twenty-year career as a very successful pirate, under the protection of powerful rulers on the Barbary Coast of Morocco. Within one year, he was putting into Sale to trim and victual his ship, and in doing so recruited another twenty-three Englishmen very keen to join him. After that he quickly built a formidable fleet capturing English, Dutch but perhaps most significantly, the pompously grand vessels of the Republic of Venice, which yielded him a huge fortune. Declining, after one rebuffed attempt to seek a pardon from King James, he ended his days as far as can be determined, a conscientious Muslim, living in a grand palace in Tunis. A wealthy and respected member of the local community, he turned his focus to the problem of incubating poultry eggs in camel dung.

One of the most powerful of all the Renegado corsairs was Murad Rais, born Jan Janz, in Harlem, Holland in the early 17th Century. In 1618 he was captured by Barbary Corsairs, near Lanzarote. Embracing Islam, he based himself in Sale and when the city declared itself an independent republic, he became chief of fourteen elected officials, the Admiral who governed the city. An outstanding and decisive leader, and an effective administrator , he raided far and wide, as a far as Reykjavik, sacked Baltimore on the Irish coast before ending his days as a Governor of Oualidia, a fortress near Sale. Again, by all accounts, he too remained a respected and admired member of the local community.

Both Captain John and Murad Rais found in Sale and Morocco an 'other' world, in which they settled and probably lived a richer life in every sense than they could have ever dreamed. More than just riches, more than power, their lives leave clues to their curiosity, adventurousness, and interests. But I wondered, as Morocco slid by, did they die content or still restless? Having left their tribe, did they ever feel they needed to belong to a new one; and did they feel they would have been accepted if they did?

By early evening I was standing in the ebb and flow of Rabat Centre Ville station, thanks to the services of a rather elegant Moroccan lady returning home from London to Fez for a holiday, a sweet elderly couple who seemed very concerned and some giggling teenage girls chaperoned by a glowering elder brother or possibly boyfriend, all of whom pushed me off and onto trains.

It was then I came face to face with the reality of a barely noticed comment in the *Lonely Planet Guide* viz that thanks to the residual historic enmity between Sale and Rabat 'petit taxis' don't ply between the different banks of the Bou Ragreb that separates the two cities and the 'grand taxis' don't call at the 'Centre Ville' station.

I wandered out in to the middle of the bustling town. The familiar feeling of 'I don't have a clue where I am' seeped into me. Standing on the corner of the street trying to make sense of the mixture of signs in Arabic and French, holding an email with the address of my destination that I was, with gathering gloom, certain that no one would have heard of, I could only think; 'Oh Bugger'. I knew what would happen next, it had happened before, in Athens, in Bangkok even in Los Angeles. Lost strangers in town exude a strange unmistakeable attractant for the false Samaritan. Someone comes up, asks you if you are English, tells you they used to work in Rotherham or Basingstoke, asks you if you support Manchester United, offers to show you how to get where you need to go, says 'let's have a coffee whilst we wait for the bus/train/friends taxi', introduces you to his 'sister' who magically appears from nowhere as equally magically he disappears, leaving you to pay $50 for the Coke you had just been sipping (Cairo) or climbing out through the toilet window to avoid the aggressive father (Athens). And this was a city, which like Sale, was built on piracy!

I retreated back to the station and the long queue of petit taxis unable to take me to my destination. Or could they? After some intense negotiation, I and the taxi driver, now known to me as Hussein, hatched a plan, one which involved an exchange of more than the normal fare. Setting off from the station we turned off the main road just before the bridge that connects Rabat with Sale and in a side street took off all the taxi signage from the battered old Renault and hid it in the back.

With our shared vocabulary of about fifty French words we slapped each other on the back and giggled at our collective cunning. A little touch of freedom already!

However, driving over the Bou Ragreb, it soon became clear, that Hussein, despite his jocularity and assurances, hadn't a clue where he was going. We circled around areas of derelict land, weaving in out of roads some of which were still under construction and others pock-marked with neglect. Every so often we would arrive back at the river accompanied by a tirade of exasperated Arabic.

In the end, I phoned the number of where I was supposed to be staying, which I had miraculously jotted down, and handed my mobile to Hussein who entered into a voluble conversation with the voice on the other end as to the best route. The conversation took some time and involved Hussein taking both hands off the wheel and pointing and waving with gusto to help the other person understand where he was. At one point he even wound down the window, tucked my mobile under his chin, and whilst driving with his knees, lent out and offered both his hands to the heavens in supplication.

As I sat in the back, I ruefully wondered whether I would end up finding pirate ghosts or joining them. With a final flourish he tossed my phone back to me and stopped the car, suddenly raising a storm of dust and protest from the driver behind. I gazed around, by the fact he was taking my bag out of the car and opening my door, I realised that this was the end of my journey. I found myself standing on the edge of a piece of wasteland with the blank wall of a row of buildings in front of me, from which little alleyways seemed to lead off. 'C'est ici,' said Hussein, shaking my hand and keeping a substantial amount of the change as a tip. 'Bonne chance!' Watching him drive off, I wondered for a second whether he had simply given up and left me on the outskirts of the old town. I had been left at what I later discovered was the old seamen's cemetery. It ran for some distance to what appeared to be an old sea wall. And so, my exploration of *A Little Nostalgia for Freedom* had begun by graves of pirates.

More prosaically, I still couldn't see where I was supposed to be staying. There was no sign on any of the buildings indicating the presence of the riad, there didn't even seem to be a front door facing me. The familiar sensation of being on the verge of catastrophe started to return. But then a smart young Moroccan walked up to me. 'Monsieur Steve?' I nodded. 'Venez-ici.'

The riad was one of those strange old buildings three or four storeys high whose dun-coloured, rendered walls impassively resist the sun and in which a single Cedar wood door opens from a narrow alley to an inner world of cool tiled floors, and interconnecting stairways leading up into a gathering dusk, all centred around a courtyard garden in which a fountain plays.

I was the only person staying there and the Moroccan who had let me in, seemed to live in the subterranean bowels of the place, so my company was very much my own. I was offered dinner a little later, and whilst I waited I opened the wooden shutters and looked out into the twilight. The riad stood on the corner of an old street, seemingly on the edge of the town. I looked out at the old cemetery and beyond it across the river to the Citadel, watching the sun go down into the Atlantic, listening to the call to prayers and the occasional bleats from the goats tethered up on the wasteland under my window. The only indication of human life was the occasional gargle of a moped as someone steered round the pot holes in the road and back into the gloom. This, I decided, was as far from home as I had felt for a long time.

The sonorous recitation of the mullah's summoning reminded me that the life of Sale has been heavily influenced by the mystical branch of Islam called Sufism. It has flourished here shaping the culture and society that developed. Sufis see the divine as something that can be directly experienced at a personal, passionate and intimate level, in other words, next-to worlds were accessible to anyone who was prepared to explore.

The outward discipline and adherence demanded by Islam is matched by an inner searching and desire to experience the ineffable. How did this fit into a pirate town?

In a state of fanciful reverie, I tried to catch the echoes of the corsairs as they walked or perhaps rode, along these alleyways to their dwellings. But such echoes were hard to catch. I wondered too about the Renegadoes, some of whom were possibly buried in the graves less than a stone's throw away.

What drove them to give up everything and be so far away from home? Was it just the lust for loot? The search must be so essential to your life to take such an irrevocable step. Surely something more than greed was at play? What was so attractive about the life of a pirate? And why the attraction to Islam? Was it the piracy or was it Islam or both? What did they both offer? *What was the essence of the freedom they chose?*

It was just that the pirates I was discovering were not like the ones I had grown up with – in fact, rather disconcertingly, they did not fit the cartoon shape that had been drawn for them.

Pirates, it seems, have been re-assessed by anarchist and socialists academic historians, as the original class warriors rebelling against an authoritarian and vicious elite. Alongside their popular repute we should set the evidence that they operated with a considerable degree of democracy, electing a captain on an annual basis; they were egalitarian: the captain was only paid about one-and-a-half times as much as an ordinary crew member; and finally, they created a sort of social insurance by which booty was taxed to provide a hardship fund for incapacitated colleagues!

Or were the Renegados entranced by the exotic mysteries of Islam? Despite the official outrage and antagonism of the Catholic Church and the whole history of conquest and reconquest between Christian and Moslem, knowledge was shared and connections existed between the wisdom of east and west made good in the backpacks of wandering scholars, and the crucibles, phials and retorts of the alchemist's cell.

And these linkages and connections, like light slipping under a bolted door, indicated a vast Islamic tradition of scientific, mathematical, spiritual and magical thinking going back over the centuries, a 'Lost History', as Michael Hamilton Morgan calls it, of extraordinary discoveries.

Couple this with a perception in the ordered Christian world, that the east was more sensual, more erotically charged than grey old buttoned-up Europe, then you have a potent sense of an esoteric and arcane knowledge which could reveal deep and tremendous things. This blend of insight and mystery became represented amongst European thinkers and occultists in the form of groups like the Rosicrucians who acted as secret societies, only revealing their knowledge step by step to initiates.

I didn't suppose the pirate Renegados were members of secret religious societies: that did seem too incongruous, but perhaps the rumours and gossip in the tavern and the quayside were a siren call. As they wandered the streets around me, were they seeking a way to find a truer self of which their everyday self was but a shadow?

A soft knock on the door summoned me dinner. I ate on my own in the central courtyard as the building rose all around me and staircases and landings with stone balustrades looked down. There were red rugs across the stone tiled floor, arches opened into rooms with red settees and dark wood furniture, softened by red and gold cushions. Lamps like baskets made of metal hung from long chains from the first floor ceiling. A tagine in its conical earthenware pot spluttered in front of me and 'Let's Face the Music and Dance' played somewhere in the house of the Barbary pirates.

CHAPTER THREE

The Eyes of a Pirate

We see things not as they are but as we are

Ancient wisdom

I awoke after a restless night's sleep in which moustachioed buccaneers on popping mopeds chased frantic goats.

Still the solitary guest, I had breakfast and waited for the arrival of Ahmed my guide for the day. I had been put in contact with Ahmed through an old friend Chris McHugo, who in a delightfully by-gone English way, seems to know everyone from the ambassador down, in Morocco. My correspondence with Ahmed before my visit had been made complicated by his shortage of English and my lack of French.

His first note to me had said: 'Dear Steve, I am a storeman, and I read many French books and I know the place of the local governments… If you pay me for passing the time with you. Why not ? Greetings.'

Several enigmatic letters later we had some sort of understanding but his last note to me had not left me confident, stating: 'Ok! I am looking forward, but you muss be tender for my English . I hope you know some French words…'

I was not convinced we were going to meet with a shared purpose, however Chris was positive that he was the man – a writer himself, very articulate (in Arabic and French particularly I suspected) and crucially, knowledgeable about Sale.

I had felt I needed someone to show me around, a local who really understood the place and could help me try to connect through the layers of culture, history and misapprehension to the vanished world of the corsair and the Renegado.

Ahmed arrived looking slightly like a timeworn Italian playboy in neat checked shirt and chinos. He seemed a dapper, intelligent-looking man with an air of rueful intelligence, and despite his relaxed dress and manner, I noticed a deeper deference compared with the guy who had let me in the previous day; and the mint tea arrived much more rapidly than my previous coffee.

'It is good to meet you, I don't know if I can help you,' he said. 'But I tell you about what I know and the pirates.'

From a battered old leather case he was carrying, he pulled out a sheaf of papers, a mixture of photocopies and handwritten notes. I realised he had decided to offer a briefing before we set off around Sale.

Ahmed's structure was somewhat circuitous; a kind of chronological exposition of the story of Sale, interspersed with ruminations on the nature of the Corsair piracy, and his own love life. Age had not dimmed his libido and he would wander off the subject of the pirates to ruminate on the numerous women with whom he had given and received pleasure.

Piecing together from his broken narrative, and things that I had previously read, a picture emerged in which the cities around the Bou Ragreb seemed to become key places of refuge for people escaping from the ebb and flow of the Muslim and Christian struggle for Spain. From the 11th Century onwards at periodic times, particularly after the re-conquest of Spain, groups of Muslims whose families had lived in Iberia for hundreds of years, arrived bewildered and angry having been expelled from their homes, livelihoods and country. Different exiles settled on either side of the river, or in an area known as the Citadel at the mouth of the river. The local Moroccans by instinct accommodated this influx, but that did not mean that their intrinsic historic independence of spirit was forgotten – in the 16th Century the parcel of land around the river managed to host three independent entities known as the Triple Republics: the present day capital Rabat, those living in the immense fortifications of the Citadel, and Sale itself. Even though this was only short-lived, Ahmed made it clear that Turkish sultans, Spanish kings and French republics and for that matter would-be Moroccan potentates never really dominated this place.

'As we like to say,' observed Ahmed. 'We keep our own keys to the house. I tell you about this place,' he said. 'The people here were not gangsters, they were fighters of the faith – this was a Jihad.' And amongst the crews were not only those born in Northern Africa, but the dispossessed of Spain thirsting for revenge and retribution. To be a Corsair, he explained, was to take part in something that was a freedom struggle, a holy war and a business operation for the citizens of the Triple Republics. The treasure was not gold, jewels and doubloons but human beings, captured in pirating expeditions as far afield as Cornwall, Ireland and even Iceland. Fleets of Corsair adventurers set sail to capture slaves, a hugely valuable prize that could be sold to provide labourers, galley slaves, servants and, from the wealthy, ransom. It is estimated that between one and one and a quarter million Europeans were seized between the 16th and 18th Centuries. Among the pirate crews of course were the Renegadoes, often choosing the third way between economic slavery in Europe and literal slavery in North Africa.

Ahmed told me you could always spot the descendants of the Renegadoes, volunteers or ex-slaves torn from the shores of Northern Europe, as many of them, unlike most Moroccans, had grey or blue eyes.

'So I show you, les Corsairs,' he said getting up and shoving the papers in my hand. 'We go!'

I stood up and put on my old battered sun hat, very aware that I did not have the haziest idea what we were going to do or see.

At one level, looking for reminders of the Corsair presence was not going to be too difficult. They are not hard to find for the pirates here were not social outcasts who ended up skewered on the end of a cutlass or hung in chains in the chilly waters of the Thames at Tilbury. The Barbary pirates were educated men who worshipped at the local mosque, studied at the local Medersa or school and were buried in personal tombs or marabouts. Men like the local hero, Mohammed Al-Ayyashi, a Corsair, scholar and local ruler who managed to enlist the help of the mighty British Navy to settle a dispute with Rabat.

So what does an old pirate town look like? The cartoons and films would have raucous bars and tumbling whorehouses jostling for position on every street. Dark corners where terrible plans are hatched, souls sold, insistent momentary lovers wrestle, deals done and broken.

But when we turned out of the riad, Sale proved to be a labyrinth of whitewashed buildings and tangled alleys wrapped around tiny squares with blank walls protecting cool interiors from the intense heat. The overall sense was quiet, dignified, restrained like a Maghrebian Cheltenham.

'I'll show you where the Corsairs went to school,' Ahmed said.

We entered a small square to one side of which was a flight of stone steps which was an entrance to the grand Mosque. At right angles to the steps was the entrance to the Medersa – L'Ecole de Corsairs, built by the command of Sultan Abu al Hassan. We stepped in through the arched door to an instant transition from breathless heat to reflective cool.

As Ahmed engaged in conversation with three raggedy looking locals one of whom came over and sold me a ticket for a few pence, I waited and looked about. Around the courtyard the lower third of the walls and pillars were simple geometric designs of small enamelled terracotta tiles of turquoise green, sandy brown and a dark reddish olive pressed into plaster. Above was a level of flax coloured, carved stucco and above this, dark-with-age wooden panels and beams of darkened Cedar that merged into the roof.

This was open at its centre to the sky. To one side a stone staircase led upstairs to some little rooms that the guide book said housed out-of-town scholars. The tone was religious, reflective, and solemn. Where were the cutlass practice rooms? Where did they learn the art of pillage?

The courtyard was not big and I stood back and tried to imagine the days when this would have been an active place of learning for the fearsome characters who would graduate from here, including the legendary Al-Ayyashi. The Medersa has the air of a sober and restrained place – something that did not really fit the essence of the carousing, swaggering bravado that maybe fancifully, seemed the personality requirement for a successful brigand. The image of the pirate as an aesthetic scholar, earnestly discussing Quaranic texts, honouring books and enquiring on moral and scientific ideas, seemed to hint at something more complex and paradoxical. It occurred to me that Corsairs and perhaps pirates in general felt able to embrace a world that did not fit together in a neat and rationally ordered way. Perhaps they were not bound so much to see the world as a jigsaw with one solution producing one picture.

Leaving the Medersa, we wandered along the near empty streets pausing to stare in at the marabouts, the mausoleums or tombs of local saints and leaders. As with many parts of the world and unlike the sanitised west, these religious sites were a typical engaging mixture of the sublime and tawdry; reverent opulence jostling for attention with poverty and dirt. These were the places that would have inspired the Corsairs, fiercely independent local saints, under whose inspiration they would set sail. As Ahmed and I peered in through the wrought iron that excluded us from the ornate tomb of Sidi Abdallah ibn Hassoun, I noticed we had been joined by a intelligent looking, scrawny guy with the vagabond appearance of an undernourished student.

Knulp?

Nonchalantly he chatted to Ahmed, replying to his questions with ease and a half-smile.

Ahmed turned to me and said: 'This man has told me about the festival they have here, once a year, they dress up as Corsairs and carry les bougies – candles – on the eve of the Prophet's birthday.'

I nodded my thanks and understanding to him. He gazed back and again I noticed the knowing smile and slightly ironic gaze. He said something else to Ahmed, who stumbled to translate.

'When he arrived, Ibn Hassoun that is, a palm tree followed, it walked behind him. It rested, put down its roots here, so this why the marabout is in this place!'

I could think of no reply beyond a nonplussed smile.

'Allez,' Ahmed indicated we should go on. But as we set off again through the honeycomb of whitewashed buildings we set off as a party of three, Ahmed deep in conversation with our self-elected guide. Emerging into the suffocating sun of midday we walked towards the sea, past the enormous cemetery I had seen from my window the night before.

More than reluctantly, as I was hoping for a gibbet or two, I was pulled in to look at another mausoleum within the graveyard. It was housed in a single-storey, rather non-descript building. From the interior, as we were about to enter, emerged a skeletal figure dressed in culottes and a dirty T-shirt. He seemed to be some sort of official guardian. I wondered for a second if I would be ejected, but he seemed content for me to enter. Peering into the single room in the middle I saw what appeared to be wooden coffin sitting on a trestle, apart from that the room was more or less bare except for some rather unpleasant looking brown marks on the wall in one corner.

The guardian explained something in Arabic. 'Al-Ayyashi's daughter is buried here,' Ahmed translated. Not in the coffin apparently but under the floor. I gazed around with what I hoped was sufficient awe, but in a low, dark dingy room housing a single coffin on a trestle and a brown stain, the flashing world of a Corsair adventurer did not seem particularly close, let alone 'next-to'.

'Look!' said Ahmed suddenly, pointing to the guardian. 'He has grey eyes. He is from Iceland, or Northern Europe, a Corsair perhaps?!' He back-translated for the guardian who looked offended and muttered a reply. 'He totally denies it, but why not?' laughed Ahmed.

Chuckling, he indicated we should go so we continued on towards the sea. As we left, our self-elected guide said something to Ahmed who looked surprised. 'You won't believe what these guardians do when there are no visitors. He says that one drinks in secret!'

At the end of the road stood the gleaming white of yet another marabout, housing the tomb of Sidi Ashar Ibn Achir. It had been a place of pilgrimage for the Corsairs, for he was known to them as the 'Doctor', and revered for his ability to quieten storms as well as the insane. I ruefully recalled that Tim Mackintosh-Smith, probably similarly frustrated, had written on the subject of visiting mausoleums in his book *Travels with a Tangerine*: "For many Muslims, it is something to be done regularly, like changing the oil in the car; it ensures the smooth running of history."

I was not allowed inside, but Ahmed asked me to wait whilst he wandered in.

'You never know, I could do with a place like this one day,' and disappeared inside.

Again I asked myself what it was I was expecting to see? I felt slightly disconnected, detached, feeling I was experiencing little but the tourist tromp. Ahmed was packaging up the experience for me, showing me the 'right things', and yet I felt a sense that there was elusive stuff behind, under and beyond the physical actuality of what I was seeing. I wondered if my approach to exploring nostalgia was just a little too fragile.

I hung around outside whilst the third member of our party sat a way off and smoked a cigarette. Peering in round corners at the entrance, I had a bizarre and friendly conversation in broken French with another guardian who looked even more skeletal and decrepit than the first. He told me he had been a pop musician. 'Moi aussi,' I smiled, to which he responded with a grin revealing some rather dubious teeth, and scratched his concave belly to indicate he had played the guitar.

Ahmed re-emerged and our third member pinched out his cigarette, pocketed it and joined us. Again he offered a little more colour to the tourist experience. Ahmed listened incredulously, seeming to check what he had heard and turned to me.

'He says, that man,' indicating the guardian who was now fortunately out of earshot, 'he fucks women at the back of the marabout! His wife, she committed suicide, just walked into the sea, kept walking, and walking till, pouf, elle n'était plus. Local guides are not usually like this,' he needlessly added.

Behind the mausoleum runs the defensive sea wall of Old Sale. It stretches around the cemetery on one side and an expanse of wasteland on the other. Built into the wall was a low building.

'This,' said Ahmed with a flourish, 'is the entrance to the old dungeons where Corsair prisoners were kept, malheureusement fermé! And ici,' he continued, pointing to the scrubland to the right, 'is where the old pirates were buried.'

Standing in the sweltering heat, looking around at the long brick wall, through which a few rusty cannons peered mournfully out to sea, the pieces of rubbish fidgeting in a slight dusty breeze, I felt more than doubtful. But what did I expect? A broken scimitar? Some rusting manacles?

I wandered over to the sea wall and peered over one of the old cannon which pointed out through a hole in the wall, to look at the beach and the rocks below, the third man talked to Ahmed. This time Ahmed looked a little embarrassed and reluctant.

'What did he say?' I demanded.

His answer was complicated, and evasively shifted between English, Arabic and French, and all the time our companion watched him with his half amused stare.

'Down there, ici, by the rocks, certain femmes, women, will kill a poulet noir, eat a special meal of couscous, cover themselves in henna, say some things and bathe at night dans la mer, this way they have children,' he concluded with a self-conscious Gallic shrug.

I looked out again at the beach trying to imagine such a thing, and the other stuff from sexual misadventure to wandering palm trees he had wanted to tell us. I wondered at the motives of our mysterious companion. Was he merely trying to entertain or was he trying to provoke something else with his brutal counterpoint of the pious with primitive and the profane. In each case, in his laconic way, he had intimated that what we were looking at, was not what it appeared. Or rather was something else as well. So it was with Knulp, I mused, this conjuring up of something beyond the mundane and given. A glimpse of freedom in the possibility of something else?

Ahmed, who seemed to be feeling things had gone too far, suddenly said: 'We go and you pay him something,' indicating our companion. I handed over some folded notes, which he put into his pocket without inspecting them, nodded his head and turned away within seconds, disappearing into the heat and the alleyways.

★

We got into Ahmed's car to drive around the perimeter of the old city wall. Half-way round we passed by the old gate through which thousands upon thousands of prisoners would have been brought, terrified, to the slave markets that lay within. It is now some distance from the water but in the past a canal had been built to enable boats from the estuary and river to be pulled up right inside the town.

According to Ahmed, miscalculations by French engineers building a break water over a century ago, had caused the Bou Ragreb to silt up and on the resulting land between the gate and the harbour, French bureaucrats had built their houses. (The history books give a different account.)

Lunch with Ahmed was long, and fascinating. We sat on the terrace of a hotel restaurant overlooking the Bou Ragreb river. Gradually our mutual franglais was improving and I began to understand a little more of his own history. It was one of resistance and a refusal to fit in. In his early years he had fought against colonial France, hiding in the mountains and taking part in vicious skirmishes that, while they did not reach the bloody levels of the civil war in Algeria, had been personal and passionate. He had been a writer, academic, general 'fixer', friend of European women and enthusiastic supporter of the Royal Family. Now he sold the houses of his friends for them and at seventy years old, still played a mean game of tennis.

It was a lunch to remember but it was with a slight feeling of frustration, of appointments somehow missed, that, late afternoon, I got back in his car to drive back to my riad. I felt as if I wasn't getting something, that some sort of insight was lurking at the periphery of my awareness.

Perhaps sensing this, Ahmed proposed stopping at a riad in the old town which he was trying to sell on behalf of the present head of one of the oldest families in Sale, and descendant of one of the great Corsair captains. Stopping the car, we picked our way down the narrow streets, passing the dark narrow workshops of wood turners, moped repairers, tailors, sellers of plastic buckets and bowls until we came to a large wooden door, wizened with age and set in a long blank wall.

Upon Ahmed's insistent knocking, the door was opened by a large, dark-haired lady who looked a little surprised to find herself greeting a member of the Sale intelligentsia, and a bearded and crumpled looking Englishman. I presumed she was some member of the family and she courteously waved us in.

After the restored opulence of the riad where I was staying, this one, although enormous and labyrinthine, was careworn and dishevelled. The little corridors we passed through on the way, opened up to rooms which were empty and unused. There were desultory signs of redecoration – a ladder leaning against a wall, an open pot of whitewash, the porcelain rubble of a broken up sink. As we entered into central courtyard space, I noticed that the floor had once had the most magnificent tiling, its fractal geometry still evident although it was now chipped and worn with age. The courtyard was not open to the heavens and the light filtered down from high above as a gloomy haze. There was stillness and a camphory smell of age.

Across the courtyard, sitting still and watching us was a tall slim lady of great age. She was dressed in a white cotton night gown (I noticed later, printed with Care Bears), white socks and a pastel headscarf. Her skin was pale and thin with age — a spirit ghost made flesh.

Pulling me into one of the other salons, Ahmed pointed to a great bed that completely crossed the end wall.

'This is where the head of the house would make fuck one of his wives – three salons, three wives a good arrangement no?' He laughed, suggestively thumping the bed. He explained a little more about the Corsair family who had lived here. They had remained one of the most important Salean families for centuries, however the latest descendant was now selling the riad as he had retired to another part of Morocco.

'I'll show you something,' he said and took me over to the salon in which the ghost sat. He pointed to a sepia photograph on the wall of a large, traditionally dressed Moroccan sitting and talking to a well-dressed European with a beaked nose and long chin.

'This man,' he said. 'He owned this place and he was the first person from Sale to open a boutique in London selling the things of artisans.' Other pictures on the wall showed him attending formal dinners with hundreds of Europeans stiff in black ties and winged collars; being interviewed on the radio, the only non European in photographs populated by men starched and shiny, and women in sparkling dresses with haughty and distant gazes.

Ahmed spoke to the lady who had shown us in, and she went and fetched some more photographs. One of them showed the old man talking to George VI and Queen Elizabeth.

'So the old Corsair eventually got to meet the King and Queen of England!' Ahmed chuckled. Suddenly, the old lady spoke in a low whisper, the photographs having stirred some memories. Ahmed listened respectfully, talking to her slowly. After a little while he turned to me.

'She says she visited London in 1935.'

That's over seventy years ago I thought. Just how old is she? I imagined her sitting here year after year, decaying gracefully with the house. There seemed to be no television or radio and even if there had been, she could not have heard it. Just memories. I wondered what would happen to her when they sold the riad; would she leave or would she finally slip into full ghosthood?

Ahmed stood up and signalled we had to go. Not sure of the protocol I nodded my head in respect to the great, great granddaughter of a Corsair pirate and noticed that she had the greyest of grey eyes.

After Ahmed has dropped me off back at the riad, I hesitated by the old front door and turned back instead down the alleyways of the old town. I felt a need to try and shape the images and passage of the day. A walk is my way, so in the just-before sense of late afternoon I let my feet take me where they would.

The formidable and imperialistic American writer, Edith Wharton, had also wandered these streets nearly a century before. Not much had changed for hundreds of years when she did so, not much has changed since.

The '*tunnelled passages where indolent merchants with bare feet crouch in their little kennels hung with richly ornamented saddlery and arms, or with slippers of pale citron leather and bright embroidered babouches*', are still there. As are the stalls with '*fruit, olives, tunny-fish, vague syrupy sweets, [and] candles for saints*'. Now Moroccan popular music sounds out from little hole-in-the-wall cafés, where two or three men with sun-wizened faces, sit on broken chairs sipping coffee and staring impassively as the world goes by, and who, what ever the accompaniment, must have also been there then as well as now.

Slavery in Sale had not been abolished until the start of the twentieth century and Edith Wharton arrived only two or three years after the French had, in her words, 'pacified' the old town. She wrote, half-admiringly of the '*ferocious old Sale·Phenecian counting-house and breeder of Barbary pirates, [where] few Christian feet had entered its walls except those, who like Robinson Crusoe, slaved for wealthy merchants in its mysterious terraced houses.*'

In this reverie, I found I had been along the Rue Ras ash-Shajara, the road on which these wealthy merchants had once lived. Emerging through an arch I stopped and looked around. I was in the Souk el-Kebir, the old slave market. In the late afternoon sun, the descendants of Berber tribesmen, Sufi mystics, Hornacheros, Mudejaresa, Moriscos and perhaps the odd Renagado were buying and selling old clothes and plastic kitchenware. These descendants traded in pots and pans in the narrow alleys and buildings in front of which once Christian captives stood and waited to be sold as slaves …

However Edith Wharton found it, dear old Sale is no longer fierce. It is sober and pious, holding raunchy Rabat at arm's length. Yet, as I stood there, head full of tombs and saints, ghosts and mystics and slaves and buccaneers my mind span in a whirl of paradoxical images that seemed to bring a complex past right into the moment of living. How to make sense of a place of: Renegadoes, slaves, the serene and civilised Medersa, the outrage of slavery, the squalor and the grandeur of the marabouts, fertility rites …?

Immersed in these thoughts and somewhat disoriented, I was not watching where I was going and bumped into someone carrying a large shrink-wrapped pallet of one litre mineral water bottles. They dropped to the ground splitting the packaging, several of the bottles rolling out under people's feet. The man, muttered at me in Arabic, whilst I tried to fashion an apology by dredging up some French. Helping him retrieve the bottles and standing up to leave him with the problem of how to carry them all, I noticed a rotund Moroccan woman in a maroon djellaba and multi-coloured headscarf watching the fun. A bark of a voice from inside one of the buildings made her start and she hurried back inside. It appeared slavery might not have totally died out here yet.

Perhaps prompted by this, as I moved away from the glare of the water carrier, I recalled a notion that I read in a book by the historian Theodore Zeldin, that of the phenomenon of 'voluntary slaves' – people who in large numbers in history have chosen to give up individual freedom to subjugate themselves to the will of another in return for protection, food, or from the fear of uncertainty itself. But surely, giving up our freedom in favour of safety and security was a shared common experience, was the very thing that many of us had done, and sometimes, nostalgically, regretted?

To rebel is to reject the expectations thrust upon us, and to conform – or even to volunteer for slavery – is to accept them. One major expectation in our subjugation seems to be that we will accept a more limited set of possibilities than the world actually affords. Another is that we will minimise uncertainty by being consistent. For inconsistency in another person is very threatening.

Time in Sale had shown me that wherever you look, the apparent seems to slide away and reveal something else. Each moment is redolent with potential.

Perhaps the Knulp-like character who had followed us had been showing us that any experience contains more than one perspective. Things are not one thing or another but rather one thing *and* another. Our moments are imbued with potential even if we don't see them.

Perhaps it is the price demanded of voluntary slavery that we accept a bolted door to alternative and richer perspectives and decide that some things and some experiences are not for us.

For the Renegados, did Sale offer the opportunity to unbolt the door and look to see what lay on the other side; a chance of sexual, religious, mystical, economic, and social liberation; the opportunity to retain some control of one's own life despite the risk? A chance to embrace more of the life not yet lived?

The Renegadoes could see a world beyond their own. In piracy they saw, not just the chance to make money but to move away from the limited and circumscribed existence in which they had been enclosed. The quintessential pirate longed to be free of rules that condemned them to a subservient and impoverished life; a sentiment perfectly captured in the words of the pirate Captain Bartholomew who, upon hearing the captain of a captured ship decline his invitation to join his crew, is reported to have said the following:

> *'You are a devilish Conscience Rascal, damn ye, I am a free Prince, and I have as much Authority to make War on the whole World, as he who has a hundred Sail of Ships at Sea, and an Army of 100,000 Men in the Field, and this my Conscience tells me; but there is no point in arguing with such snivelling Puppies, who allow Superiors to kick them about the Deck at Pleasure'*

Perhaps the more subtle Renegadoes could also see beyond their social imprisonment, that in the exotic mysteries of Islam, particularly in the arcane Sufi elements which so shaped the consciousness of Sale, were clues to a richer and deeper world, that we all sense but turn away from. To enter this world requires letting go of the assumptions that keep us in our place today. It also means we have to be more 'experimental' with ourselves, not demanding we should be always as we ever were.

Why is this so difficult? Perhaps because the tribal part of us has a fear of the ambiguous, an aversion to the inherent contradictions of people, place and moment, and a kind of dread of appearing inconsistent?

Was this part of what nostalgia was all about? Were the doctor, and the tailor, the smith and the tanner to whom Knulp was so important, voluntary slaves? Had these good German burghers surrendered their freedom, as thousands of us have in factories, bureaucracies and corporations in return for the appearance of a safer, more ordered life and social standing? In a world of possibilities, are we encouraged overtly and covertly to choose the safer options and stick to them? Is being reminded of the denied potential for a richer more complex life one source of our nostalgia? This would be mourning not just for the more exciting road not taken but for willingly fencing ourselves off from the broad possibilities of a moment.

As I turned back from the old slave market to return to my lodgings, I wryly recalled Zeldin's assertion that statistically most of us would be descended from slaves.

Back in my room I stared once more through the window as the evening light faded on the sea, the Citadel and the mournful old goat still tethered outside. It faded too on a long day closing. A day which had unfolded itself, revealed itself, side stepped, shimmied and promenaded around what is and what is not. Sale had turned out to be a shape shifter of a place. It is the austere, unbending cleric, the sea wolf, the grotesque, and the ghost.

All four and more – at the same time.

'*Sale, and probably the world,*' I thought to myself and the ghost of Knulp, *'is best understood to be about the possible and irreconcilable, not the neat and definitive.'*

'There is always more behind what you think you see,' said the voice of Knulp. 'I guess it is the soil in which you have been cultivated, predisposes you to think there is a proper way of seeing things, of understanding things, a right answer, a best argument.'

I guess that is a pragmatic way of dealing with the world, I thought. It is also a social, perhaps a tribal one. In order for a tribe to work, it requires that on the whole you see and value things in much the same way as do others in the tribe.

'But perhaps it is not a *complete* way of seeing things,' said Knulp.

'Is there such a thing?' I wondered.

Sale had reminded me that the world is messy. A single question can have many responses to it all of which are a partial answer depending on how you understand the question. Were the Corsairs good? Does water boil at 100 degrees; what caused the Economic Crisis etc? Such questions can have several different answers depending upon the perspective and purpose of both who asks the questions and who answers it.

As the sun glittered on the water, I suspected that the impulse of the pirate and the Renegado is within us all, and that a nostalgia for freedom is fashioned when we see the world not as limited and limiting, but imbued with potential, paradox and prospect.

And the mirror of this is our internal world. Pirate life is seen as unfettered, unrestrained, seeming to lack principle. But it was also disciplined, structured and shaped by code and belief. The freedom of the pirate is to embrace this inconsistency and the inevitability of change it implies.

The voluntary slave, meanwhile, tries and fails to deny this ambiguity by trying not to see it. If we believe, I mused, there is ultimately a right and single way of seeing things and that way is one we have learned as a member of our family or our tribe, then we accept a particular interpretation of the messy world and bind ourselves to it. We also bind ourselves within it, I had decided. Our tribal upbringings teach us how the world is and we behave in our place in it.

The freedom of the pirate is not to cast off from one sort of world and sail completely into another, but navigate in both waters and to embrace the impossibility of this, makes us who we are.

'That's the way it is,' said Knulp. 'Being a voluntary slave or a pirate are different ways of responding to the same challenge.'

What shapes the way we respond I wondered?

A curious day I thought, as the streets quietened in preparation for the evening call to prayers. Thinking about it – I hadn't found what I was looking for, I had found something else. It required a different kind of looking to find something you were not looking for.

But I had an early start, the Moroccan train timetable to Marrakech to confront and a mountain to think upon.

CHAPTER FOUR

The Mud of Morocco

Down in the hearts of us we are vagabonds all, if not by occasional habit, at least by inclination

RS Spittel, Wild Ceylon

So was I pirate with a hidden voluntary slave, or a voluntary slave harbouring brigandish tendencies? I mused.

'Perhaps it depends upon the moon?' said Knulp.

I lay in my room in the tower of the Kasbah du Toubkal. Outside I could hear the sounds of the Imlil valley, the shout of a mule boy to his reluctant beast, the last fading cry of the call to prayer, the muted roar of a waterfall mingling with the chirrup of the stream, the half-hearted crow of a cockerel.

A shaft of the late afternoon sunlight shone through the closed wooden shutters and the dust danced in the beam. I playfully tapped the blanket on which I lay and watched a thousand miniature stars of dust-light float and swirl up into the air above me. Each a potential robber of my breath, they danced, wandered and skimmed on unseen wavelets of warm air... 'They be like little angels' an imaginary voice said in my ear, for some reason with a Dorset accent.

I raised my hand into the sunbeam and the 'angels' disappeared. Amused I raised and lowered my hand again making them vanish and reappear. This, what the psychologists call displacement activity, was probably a result of the following day's plans to set off on a solo trek through the High Atlas Mountains.

My notion was that the restless nostalgia that Knulp provoked was not just wanderlust, but that wanderlust was itself a locomotive version of something deeper, taking a glimpse through Knulp's eyes seemed essential. I wondered if part of the magic of Knulp was the fact that he was constantly on the move. And if so, what was it that we part-time voluntary slaves sense he gains from this.

We are mostly descended from Nomads. Apparently our Neanderthal ancestors were more sedentary and tended not to wander too far. And now they are no more. Were they less restless and therefore didn't survive? Perhaps the stimulation travel offers has a contribution to our survival.

The point was to experience at least a little, the rewards of the Knulp the wanderer. Bruce Chatwin, the celebrated journeyer, promises:

> 'the act of journeying contributes towards a sense of physical and mental well-being, while the monotony of prolonged settlement or regular work weaves patterns in the brain that engender fatigue and a personal sense of inadequacy!'

OK Brucie, but why?

I have some great friends who do the explorer/adventurer stuff. People like Barry Roberts, climber and explorer who recently fought off a polar bear attack in Greenland with a saucepan, Stephen Venables, who was the first Briton to climb Everest without oxygen and Robert Twigger, who crossed Canada in a birch bark canoe.

But I am not one of them.

A little overweight, I am more used to a bit of sailing, the odd ascent of a modest rock in the Derbyshire Hills; more comfortable with a glass of wine than a compass, a guitar than a rucksack, a book than a bivouac. So, not for me a mad jaunt across the snowy Arctic wastes, or grimly hanging onto a rope dangling from the roofs of heaven over a craggy drop. Nor for me either was sixteen months living in the bush eating grubs and drinking whisky with the last of the *Whatdoyoucallthem* tribe.

Tough is a relative proposition, and what Baz, Stephen and Twigger would find a Sunday stroll, I knew I would find a little more intimidating. My journey would be here in the High Atlas Mountains on a four-five day trek with my friend 'Brahim, a Berber guide. Its end would be a tromp up Mount Toubkal, the highest peak in North Africa, with some friends who were flying out later from England. The first part however was to take a vague circular route over the steep-sided valleys and passes where awe-generating bare, rugged peaks and faces descend sharply down through pocket terraces of barley to lush but narrow orchards of apple and fruit trees – starting and ending at the Kasbah.

The Kasbah is situated on top of a small hill above the Berber village of Imlil, on the route up to Toubkal. It is one of my favourite places. The inspiration of Mike McHugo whose brother had located Ahmed for me, it is the renovated summer palace of the old Caid who ran these parts during the era of the French protectorate, and was still torturing people within its walls as late as 1946. It is run in collaboration with the local village association which it helped to create. In a place where electricity only arrived a few years ago, the road can be washed away by spring torrents, medical care is limited and there is very little infrastructure, it has been a catalyst for positive change. Not only does it only employ local craftsmen in its renovation and local people to run it but it taxes itself a voluntary 5% of revenue to support village projects. I've been visiting the Kasbah for over ten years and have grown very fond of the place. You can't really call it a hotel. They call it a Berber hospitality centre and it is, Very.

So it had been with a feeling of returning to the loved and familiar, I was rescued by a couple of amiable members of the staff upon my arrival in Marrakech and brought to Imlil. From here I had got on a mule and on a black and starry night rode up the windy rocky path amongst the walnut trees to the gate of the Kasbah. All around me, sensed as much as seen, the towering snow covered summits of the Atlas Mountains loomed.

As usual Abdu greeted me as I removed my shoes and entered the main part of the Kasbah. Abdu is the brother of Haj Maurice, the diminutive but authoritative figure whose word seems final around here. Abdu is the fixer who runs the things on a day to day basis.

'Hello Stiv, welcome, welcome – everything is good?'

'Everything is good Abdu, and I am pleased to see you!' I replied.

'Tomorrow you stay here my friend and rest. 'Brahim is ready, I fix everything, then you go the next day. You will eat?'

So I had spent the day wandering around the Kasbah, reading a book, making a few notes in my Moleskine notebook. Since my trip to Sale I had been thinking about 'voluntary slavery'. Was this too strong a term to describe how many of us live our lives? Could we be so uncertain of ourselves that we bind ourselves to less than we might be?

Zeldin noted there were different sorts of voluntary slavery. People volunteered to be slaves in Russia, Aztec Mexico and elsewhere as a kind of social welfare system. They surrendered their freedom for food, accommodation protection. Between the 15th and 18th Century in old Russia there were more voluntary slaves than there were townspeople, priests or soldiers. Another even more insidious form of voluntary slavery is what Zeldin provocatively describes as 'the ancestor of today's ambitious executive and bureaucrat'. Throughout history, wealthy and powerful people wanted to be seen as not working. It was demeaning to work and so they created bureaucracies of slaves to do it for them. Ironically in some situations such slaves could gain considerable status relative to each other and become powerful, particularly in societies like the Ottoman and Chinese empires.

Now Knulp was very good at 'not working', he had built a

lifestyle out of it but 'not working' was not the whole story because then nostalgia would be much created by someone who was idle and very rich, rather than a poor vagabond. Clearly, I thought, as the dust sparkled in the afternoon sunshine and I massacred and resurrected angels, there is something about the fact that Knulp was constantly travelling. What is the allure of a vagabond beyond a temporary scent of freedom for a voluntary slave?

The following morning I was standing at the gates of the Kasbah du Toubkal eyeing up an old mule laden with tents, bottles of water, sleeping bags, pots, pans and my rucksack which had mysteriously disappeared before breakfast that morning, pushed into great raffia baskets strung on either side of the beast. As usual Abdu's preparation was thorough and complete.

With his customary grin 'Brahim appeared lolloping up towards me from the valley below.

'Hey Steve, how are you?' 'Brahim is every inch the modern Berber guide. Police sunglasses, pushed back into black curly hair, quality trekkers and, a near permanent grin on his face – and excellent English, if a little idiosyncratically shaped by being learned from British trekkers from Basingstoke and Brentford.

'Are you ready for this?' When I nodded my assent. 'Fanta plastic!'

Abdu waived us good bye with a final 'Everything is good?' and we set off down the hill from the Kasbah and through the village past open 'boutiques' selling carpets, shoes, trinkets, pieces of quartz and other rocks. As we passed them, boys in grubby jumpers and even scarves despite the heat pleaded with me to step inside.

'Just quick look, no pressure.'

They were dismissed by 'Brahim with either a smile or curt wave of the hand depending I supposed on past mutual history.

We turned right at the bottom of the hill and stopped in a little rough square. About twenty mules shifted nonchalantly around whilst one poor beast was loaded up with a vast amount of gear including: gas bottles, carpets, blue plastic barrels, boxes of bottled water, tarpaulins, a fold-down chair and what seemed to be a box of vegetables. Two mules boys, supervised by a smiling rotund man, pushed, shoved and shouldered stuff into the two huge wickerwork panniers that hung on either side of the beast. They tied things in place with frayed lengths of yellow plastic raffia string.

'Brahim walked over to the supervisor shaking hands and touching his heart in that typical Moroccan way. Their conversation seemed to go a while, and I grew restless to get going until it dawned on me they were waiting for the boys to finish packing. It also became apparent that the second mule was coming with us as well as were, it soon transpired, the mule boys and the supervisor, who I now knew as Mohammed the cook. Abdu was going for gold.

So, feeling a bit of a fraud, my 'solo' trek consisting of a guide, a cook, three muleteers, two mules and me, set off from the dust, heat and noise of Imlil to take a long, very steep and very rocky path up a pass to the east of us and cross into the next valley.

It was a warm day and at first the going was tough but 'Brahim soon taught me the Berber plod. Employing the basic physics of gradient and stride he insisted that I should shorten my step the steeper the incline.

'Baby steps Steve and slowww, but don't stop, ziggy-zag but don't stop!' Sometimes he would tactfully walk in front of me if he thought my stride was too long or my pace too quick. Looking back, it has become a lesson for life. If the going gets tough take shorter steps but don't stop!

By late lunchtime we had reached the top of the pass. We paused to eat. The aspect was magnificent. The High Atlas is a landscape weathered and broken by time. Altitude defines it. The summits are bare, precipitous and where the gradient is less than perpendicular, still covered in snow. Further down, once wooded slopes are barren and brutalised and Rowan and Juniper bushes cling to the scree. Yet further down still, a miracle occurs. Terraces green with early barley, little dining table-sized plots of vegetables, cluster between tiny orchards of cherry and apple that sink down towards sparkling streams. There is spirit in this landscape. The terraces are centuries old and still being renewed. The very soil is hand-made. Silt is collected from streams and mixed with animal waste spread upon the terraces. The silt also provides the basic ingredient for the mudbricks from which the little Berber villages, streets no wider than a mule with well filled panniers and clinging to the valley sides, are made.

Whilst I sat on a rock and took in the view, the rest of the expedition party laid out a carpet, fixed together a rusty old stove, and started cooking. Lunch, when it was served, consisted of a sort of salad of chopped tomatoes, peppers, red onions, cucumber, tinned tuna and, astonishingly, hot meatballs cooked with pepper and spices. This was accompanied by loaves of flat bread, water and coffee.

It was a feast. At the top of the pass was a little stone hut where a man spent all day waiting for the occasional traveller to come by who might want to buy the warm can of Coke which he kept on the window ledge. Not surprisingly, enticed by the smell of the food he wandered over. Amiably, people moved over and indicated that he should join us. He sat down and was handed a tin plate.

After eating, I lay back on the carpet and stared in to the big blue sky. This was perfect. Knulp was onto something.

But if this wasn't completely perfect, the next second was. 'Brahim shook my shoulder and pointed. Swooping up the pass, circling over on a soaring glide that distained any wing movement, was a majestic Golden Eagle. It came amazingly close, close enough to see the fierce, imperious look in its eyes and to imagine the downdraft from its wings had touched our cheeks.

'Oopsy daisy. It is a good sign,' said 'Brahim. Although of what, he did not say. It flew above us for a couple of minutes, perhaps considering whether to join us, and then tipped its wings and slid out of sight into the next valley. Actually I don't know if it was for a couple of minutes or half an hour. Time had paused and held its breath.

The spell broken, we re-packed the mules and set off down the other side of the pass and pressed on. By late afternoon we arrived at a flat piece of land near the head of the valley. As the sun dropped behind the mountains, the air rapidly cooled. I was given a little mountain tent to sleep in and another much larger tent was erected a little way away. This was the cook tent and the tent for the others to bed down in.

That night we all sat together in the cook tent eating a tagine of lamb and vegetables after a bowl of soup. It was warm and companiable inside the tent. Only 'Brahim had the distinction of speaking both Berber and English, so valiantly struggled as an interpreter. For some reason they were intrigued by the relationship between the French and the English. There followed a bizarre conversation in which I, via 'Brahim, tried to explain the origins of the English language and the Hundred Years War.

At about 8.30 the combination of altitude and exertion made me unbelievably weary. Bidding the others good night, I crawled into my tent. As I lay in my sleeping bag I suddenly remembered that I had not looked at the photographs of the Golden Eagle as it a soared overhead. I got out my camera and looked at the images I had taken. I was bitterly disappointed. Here was no flying predator captured in a frozen grandeur that could evoke a heady mix of exhilaration, threat and joy. No, my camera had seen only an eagle-shaped sparrow lost on a two dimensional background. I felt in a strange way cheated as if some vital evidence had been stolen from me. I ruefully recalled HM Tomlinson's remark about the impossibility of capturing an experience. He'd written: *'The rewards of travel, which make it* worthwhile[1], *cannot be accounted beforehand and are seldom matters a listener would care to hear about afterwards, for they*

---

1 My emphasis

have no substance, they are no matter. They are untranslatable from time and place'.

Is this something we sense about Knulp, that he experiences more of these fragile moments or even experiences them more completely? He has the time and the perspective to be present. In his state of freedom, time is his resource and no one else's. He is unlike the hordes of frantic tourists desperately seeking to capture the beauty of a moment through a camera lens, hoping to consume the experience later but finding it a thin gruel made from the remnants of a rich dish.

I remembered Knulp had remarked that the most beautiful things filled him with compassion, even sadness as well as pleasure, for they are in some sense momentary, the warmth in their beauty comes from their impermanence. He had likened it to watching an exquisite firework; at its greatest moment its end begins. Beauty that is permanent, he thought, was 'colder.'

For a few days we criss-crossed the passes and valleys of the region, camping out in deserted valleys and the crest of mountain passes. I had worried about my fitness but apart from a mild headache that disappeared by day two, I felt fine.

I had come on this trip from a stressful and complex existence and noticed I was becoming increasingly relaxed. My life at that time was an impossible intersection of competing goals and demands. Dealing with them here was impossible and they quickly faded to a vague zero. Travelling by foot I noticed has a simplifying effect. When the goal in front of you is a steep 500m ascent and a blistering hot day then more intangible goals and worries tend to be in full retreat. The effect was amazingly liberating. When daily life becomes the pursuit of a limited number of clear simple goals then I could see how the past, present and future rebalance themselves. I could also see how it was possible to pursue more audaciously a dream of the life you wanted to live when you weren't dragging around a sack full of competing goals.

I mused on the causes of my new found state of mind. At walking pace life grows in intensity and richness. You notice things or see them more completely. For instance take the mud. The mud of Morocco isn't brown at least not in the Atlas Mountains. In the High Atlas Mountains it is cinnamon, ochre, olive, purple, khaki, red as rust, even blue as egg shells. Yet until yesterday I would have called it brown. I remembered some psychological research that showed that walking improved our ability to perceive things and discriminate detail.[2] Was it fanciful I wondered to imagine that it also makes social perception more discriminatory, helping us to see what is really important.

Once I took tea with the 'mayor', as 'Brahim described him, of a local village of mudwalled dwellings. On the roof terrace of the dwelling that he runs as a kind of very basic guest house, he sat in a blue djellbah and went through the elaborate ritual of preparing mint tea. Water was boiled in an old kettle containing a twig of mint leaves over a small fire in a clay pot. At a suitable point the twig was removed and then contents of the kettle were poured into a glass. Sometimes the contents were discarded and sometimes poured back into the kettle. When the liquid was sufficiently clear, broken up pieces of sugar chipped from a rock of the stuff was added. Again the liquid was poured from kettle to glass and back again each time with a rising motion of his arm so that the liquid travelled through the air into glass. Eventually he seemed satisfied with the whole procedure and tea was served. The whole process took nearly half an hour.

Another time we descended from a high pass into a miniature Eden of cherry trees, red with fruit and shimmering with the particular light that is the alchemic combinations of sun, green leaves teased by a breeze and tumbling clear water. Washing clothes on a bolder-strewn waterfall, four beautiful Berber women with

---

2 When Walking Makes Perception Better; Frank H Durgin, Current Directions in Psychology Science , Vol 18, Number 1 Feb 2009

fine features and bright clothes and head scarves the colour of turmeric and burgundy, were lost in the timeless light intimacy that alleviates a domestic chore. Through 'Brahim, I asked if I could take their photograph. Smiling they refused, worried they would end up on a postcard being sold in Marrakech.

Each of these scenes, and several others, had a kind of completeness, a sort of momentary fragile perfection. '*Untranslatable from time and place*'.

But I also started to see that the walking pace of travel invited you not just to observe the fleeting and unfolding moment, but to be involved in it, shaping the experience. I could acknowledge how little I was usually present in the experience of the moment. Not just in a kind of popular meditative sitting still sort of way, passively acknowledging the unfolding present, but in the intense involvement that a musician brings to a performance, a potter to fashioning shape from clay, lovers to the pursuit of ecstasy. Being actively present probably takes a kind a special kind of intelligence.

One morning we had got up early and climbed to the top of a plateau that offered the most wide and dramatic view of the mountains disappearing into infinity. The pleasure of the sight was seasoned by the knowledge offered by 'Brahim that no one had seen this view for many years as the old shepherds path that used to guide the route had been washed away.

By the time we had scrambled down the thousand or so metres to the top of the pass that crossed the mountains, I began to feel weary. It was lunch time and I lay on a bed roll under a tree. Without moving I watched the cook, helped by one of the mule boys, prepare lunch. Over the course of the trek I had grown to appreciate the total engagement and commitment brought to the job of trekking, particularly the preparation of food by these guys. Despite the roughest of tools and utensils there was an evident pleasure and commitment in doing these things with grace and assiduousness. It was a quality I would also see later in Saleh, a

Bedouin in the Sahara who showed a fastidious care in everything he did; from making a lentil soup in a battered cook pot, baking flat bread on a piece of old metal over the smouldering embers of a fire, cleaning the most distressed of ancient pans till they shone or combing his hair and tying his shemagh with the attention to detail of a haute couture milliner.

This was an echo of Knulp. Being immersed in doing the small things well his friends noticed was an essential part of who he was. They noticed and appreciated his fine manners and the care and consideration in which he did everything. Even eating a sausage: '*After neatly removing the skin and setting it aside on his plate, he slowly and with visible relish spread the soft sausage on his bread. From time to time he took a swallow of the good yellow cider. The tanner looked on in appreciation as Knulp's slender delicate hands went through the motions so neatly and easily and the lady of the house also took pleasure in watching him*'.

Being absorbed is itself a magical place. People talk about being present, in the moment, being in the 'now', but it is this and more. It is more than real. The usual boundaries are altered as we are captivated in a distorted present in which detail becomes magnified and more tangible but in which context as well as past and future become shadowier and more ephemeral. Is this why it is such a compelling, albeit temporary relief, from our voluntary slavery?

As I lay on the ground, head propped up on my rucksack, I recalled a moment sitting on the balcony of a fading once-grand hotel, gazing at the way late afternoon sun played across the roofs of the town, to back inside the hotel room where a beautiful half-naked woman sat at a dressing table and in practised, expert reverie applied her make-up.

A particular moment is capable of holding almost infinite sensations, emotions and resonance. A moment can echo and haunt, being present opens up that moment's complexity and contradictions.

Knulp reminds us that our nostalgia is also for the freedom to immerse ourselves in the richness of a moment and to touch for a second, a transitory, impermanent next-to-world of possibility: a moment to reconnect with the prospect of who we might be.

Is the freedom of the vagabond and the wanderer I wondered, to experience life through fewer, more observed steps, taken at a 'Berber plod' which in some way makes the very rewards of the future we might be chasing, present in the 'now'? The riches we dream of are in some sense, implicit in the present. Is this one way we voluntary slaves can be freed from the tyranny of ancient obligation and future consequence, to experiment with our potential?

My reverie was suddenly interrupted by the arrival of a flock of little black goats and their minders; two old men and a boy. They, without seeming invitation, sat down to eat. I was too knackered to do the multi-cultural bit so I just waived feebly at them. I wondered how at each meal different shepherds had appeared out of nowhere within minutes of us stopping and wryly recalled the story of Wilfred Thesiger crossing the great Empty Quarter. After a few days of stopping and feeding considerable numbers of Bedouin, who seemed just to emerge from the desolation from time to time, he began to suspect there was an entire tribe tracking him just out of view.

One morning 'Brahim and I sat for nearly forty minutes on the large rock on a path watching a group of men and boys trying to free a mule laden with so much hay that its panniers had become wedged between the walls of the single file bridge – a bridge we needed to cross sometime.

As they sweated, pushed and pulled and the animal wouldn't, couldn't move, we chatted.

'Are Berber people content?' I asked him. He thought about it.

'We are very "tranquil",' he said.

A description of 'Brahim himself I thought. There was a strength about him. A kind of certainty. He is a man with an encyclopaedic knowledge of the plants, animals, birds of the Atlas Mountains, a skilful guide who never seems to get tired or frustrated with the plodding company of puffing westerners. Curious, talkative, thoughtful. Strong, I thought not in a physical sense, or even in terms of courage. A word sprang to mind: strong in terms of fidelity. He is true to himself. Faithful. Tranquil. I wondered if this were true of some of the Corsairs, of Knulp?

'We are very independent but also we look after each other,' he continued. 'It is both.'

He gave the example of the little irrigation channels than run at right angles along the sides of the hills. Jointly constructed by the local village, a series of primitive sluice gates open the water into different fields. By mutual agreement different farmers open the gates to their fields on different days of the week ensuring everyone gets a fair share of the water.

Similarly, the local muleteers operate a system by which they elect a chief who organises who works when, so that everyone gets a fair share of the opportunity. The chief also takes a levy on money earned to share out amongst those who do not work and to support anyone whose mule 'breaks down'. He also is the judge in any dispute between them.

As we walked, 'Brahim had already tried to explain to me more about the Berbers. He claimed that they originally were a tribe from Germany. I suppose I didn't really believe him until early one morning I grasped a steaming mug of coffee and stared bleary-eyed across a stream. In a valley some way up on the other side, some Berber families had established a camp for their summer pastures. To my surprise, a pretty girl with the palest of skin and beautiful red hair that tumbled half way down her back, came skipping up the stream and started to climb the hill on the otherside. Incongruously she was wearing the bright burgundy and saffron dress typical of local women. She looked so European that I speculated that she must be the daughter of a French couple we met trekking the previous day, dressed up in kind of ethnic chic. I looked around for her parents but there was no sign of them and then I realised she had disappeared amongst the goats and rough dwellings in front of me. 'Brahim appeared from amongst our own mules and I questioned him about what I had seen.

'But she is typical,' he said looking earnestly out from beneath his black curly hair. 'Many Berber people have hair this colour and skin too.'

'But not you,' I said.

'No, not me.'

The thing I keep discovering about Morocco is that 'typical' has an elusive quality.

I later found out that the Berber word for Berber is 'Imazighen' which is derived from an old word meaning free and possibly noble. In fact the scholars who propose this translation also propose that these words are 'the closest we can come to a universal Berber trait' and noted amongst the Berber peoples 'the emphasis on freedom and the apparent absence of a state'. For centuries Berbers across North Africa have had a reputation for tough independence and a refusal to become bound by a nation or much in the way of civic organisation, yet at the same time can operate on a personal level with a transcendent degree of cooperation and harmony.

Through 'Brahim, meeting others Berbers and reading about them, my impression is of a people who live quite easily with uncertainty. Perhaps it is the harsh environments in which they have always dwelt, from the Tuareg warriors of the desert to the proud people of the High Atlas whom the French failed to bring under colonial control. But Berbers seem to move to their own drumbeat, adapting to changing conditions or simply ignoring them.

Was it coincidence that Knulp led me here on a search for freedom to a people who are defined by it? There were clear echoes here between what I had seen in Sale – a seemingly natural human tension between fitting in and falling out in the way we manage our lives. And I was developing a strong sense that the ability to be actively engaged in the magic of the here and now was relevant to the way we deal with and try to resolve this tension.

And to do this perhaps meant accepting the irresolvable, letting opposites co-exist as natural, albeit antagonistic, bedfellows – the vagabond and the voluntary slave dissolving them in the freedom of now.

CHAPTER FIVE

The Boy Who Belonged to Himself

Once upon a time there was a funny dog, called Crispin's Crispian.
He was named Crispin's Crispian because he belonged to himself...
one morning he didn't know where he wanted to go.
'Just walk and sooner or later you'll get somewhere,'
he said to himself
Margaret Wise Brown, Mister Dog

After several days ascending and descending the Atlas Mountains in a huge circle, of which the Kasbah was the epicentre, we headed back. We crossed a pass called the Tizi Mzik and walked a curving path across the scree and rubble back down into the valley of Imlil. By now the back of my hands were burned from using walking poles, I was filthy with several layers of Moroccan mud and grit and my legs were weary with continuously breaking myself against the incline. My head hurt, probably from a mixture of slight dehydration and altitude but I was profoundly content.

It seemed easy walking down through the lazy sounds of an early morning in the mountains to recognise that in the frenetic lives we lead, spending our hours building our defences against future disaster, we lose the simplicity that allows a state of being that is actively engaged with the world in front of and around us.

'*Hanging on in quiet desperation*' as Pink Floyd used to say, is not a good place from which to admire the view. So Knulp, the traveller, evokes that old memory of the freedom of the road. Paradoxically perhaps, this is the freedom *not* to have a destination, or even several competing 'destinations', but more simply, a freedom to be in the unfolding moment. A freedom to be engaged in the emerging possibilities of ourselves.

On such a tide I arrived back into the Kasbah, through the arch door of its entrance and into the little oasis garden of trees, languid pools of water, shrubs and brightly coloured flowers that lies at its centre. A couple of American tourists, his face shiny pink, hers bottled gold and apricot, were looking dubiously at some of Abdu's walking poles. Abdu saw me and grinned.

'Welcome back Steve, everything is good?'

'Fantaplastic, Abdu,' I said. 'Fantaplastic.'

'Your friends will arrive soon, I will make them welcome – all is ready.'

Taking advantage of a mutual piece of work, the following week some friends were joining me and we planned to take a couple of days off and walk up Mt. Toubkal. As well as Hugo with his booming voice fresh from Tunbridge Wells in the UK, there would be Jonathan, an Australian former world class canoeist and my friend and colleague Marie.

The plan was that they would arrive later in the day and then early the next morning we would set off first to the refuge at the foot of Toubkal and then, with a very early start, the ascent of the mountain itself. I knew that the arrival of these good friends would mean a resumption of the constant banter and teasing that signals affection and friendship in the west. With my head noisy with thoughts and in body, knackered and beyond thinking, in preparation, I found a shady spot on the roof terrace and fell fast asleep.

'Steve, you're snoring!' I awoke to find myself staring at the feet of Hugo Pound.

'Hello Hugely,' I yawned. 'So you've got here!'

My fellow would-be mountaineers gazed down as I groggily

raised myself from my sleep. It felt odd meeting them here, my brain was still up in the mountains. They are good supportive friends in that gently mocking English sort of way, Marie in a particular, has pulled me out of more than one metaphorical ditch over the years. Yet at this moment they looked different, foreign even, or rather mysteriously familiar as if you know something is different but can't put your finger on it.

That evening we sat in the central hall of the old Kasbah, dimly lit by candles and caught up with each other. The oddness of seeing them wore off through the typical and ageless dancing interplay of dialogue and the convivial circling of old stories and points of view through which old friends re-connect and make their plans.

Early next morning, with the benefit for my friends as well as myself of a bath and a good night's sleep, we set off up the mountains. Again we were accompanied by Abdu's entourage including a mule with a wonky eye and lolling tongue to whom we gave the name Florence.

The walk up to the refuge, from where we would set off for the climb to the summit the following day, was long but steady. 'Brahim led the way again, insisting on a regular pace.

'Take it easy-peasy, lemon squeezy.' So we rolled along at a good pace, Florence and her compatriots bringing up the rear with their jangling panniers of pots, pans and kettles.

On the way up we passed through a little clump of dwellings, Sidi Chamharouch. The locals here would fish for trekkers slogging up to Toubkal or with a less pazazz, offer sustenance and support to pilgrims to a local hermitage where women who were struggling to conceive or who were ailing, would go to pray for help. The hermitage is a group of squat buildings gathered around a large, incongruously white boulder, as if a giant meteorite from the heavens had crashed into the dun and dusty landscape.

Morocco is dotted with such places, often inhabited by still living saints, descendants of generations of the same, whose purpose was to provide a link between the everyday and the arcane for small isolated communities. I had spoken to one of the local men about the hermitage but he was almost dismissive of it. It's not an important thing he had wanted to say, it's really no matter.

But it did matter, it was a destination for women in a region where the twin worlds of men and women rarely met, the women dominating the inside world of home, a parallel world to the outside more Islamicised world of men. Parallel worlds, described by one group of authors as 'women/magic/sanctuary and men/ Islam/mosque reflecting a "dual soul" in Berber society'.

'Brahim trotted up, riding a mule Berber style, sitting on the beast's shoulders, legs dangling over the same side. He was less divisive.

'It is a good place,' he said' 'Very tranquil.'

We continued along a path that leads alongside a stream and runs steeply uphill to the right side of the Isougouane valley. By now, somewhat used to 'Le Grand Expedition' nature of trekking with Abdu as the jolly quarter master and 'Brahim as the munificent major, I was not surprised when at lunch time a carpet was rolled out on a rocky terrace, four white canvas chairs erected and a table laid. However, even I raised an eyebrow when a bottle of Moroccan white wine was produced and four glasses set out. My colleagues were astonished. Marie whose natural toughness is no bar to her accepting unexpected luxury, settled into the swing of a three course lunch. Jonathan and Hugo were not so relaxed: giggles at the incongruity of it all alternating with giggles of embarrassment as earnest trekkers, clad in Lycra and carrying mini aerodynamic backpacks, strode purposefully past. Sitting in Victorian splendour at the side of a path eating Spanish omelette, drinking a glass of white wine chilled in a thundering stream of melt water, whilst being grunted at by tough looking passers-by sucking on straws of energy drink was clearly not in the pre-event visualisations.

Gradually we made our way up the valley to the refuge – a large, damp place built in the French style of mountain adventure to winnow out the faint-hearted and hygiene conscious. After another enormous meal prepared by Abdu's relentless victualling, we crashed out on broad bunks along with thirty to forty other people. A restless night ensued with furious accusations of snoring and worse being exchanged until a cold grey dawn broke to provide a kind of relief and groggily we set off.

Basically once you are used to the altitude, climbing up Mount Toubkal is a steady plod. For us, patches and more extensive fields of snow added to the adventure. As we alternated between jokey banter and the grimly silent exertion of the more intimidating bits, we told each other anecdotes and stories, the little moments of personal biography which offer as explanation for why we get out of breath, why we need to walk in single file, why 'Brahim's strange singing provokes an unexpected memory, why 'this reminds me of that.' Marie, at best of medium height, reminisced about wanting to join the Tank Corps, Hugo about his time as a chorister at public school and Jonathan derry-doing in the rain swept hills of Tasmania.

'Tell us about your wife and how you met,' Marie asked 'Brahim suddenly, partly I guess to distract him from his relentless, jolly quarter-note chanson. And he did.

His father one day had told him: 'It is time you got married son.' He took his father seriously. A few days later he was returning from a trip guiding trekkers across the mountains. A girl was working planting vegetables in the family garden. 'Brahim looked at her and found her beautiful. So ignoring preamble and prevarication and despite having never met her before, said: 'Hello, will you marry me?'

And she looked at him and said: 'You had better send your father around to my father to talk about it.' And that was that.

Around ten o 'clock, the sun now high in the sky and the air crystal clear, we stopped for a rest. I sat on a rock a little way from the others. Facing west the mountains marched into what seemed like an infinite distance but what was probably forty miles to the start of the coastal plain. I enjoyed the fact of believing (correctly) that in that distance there was probably nothing more than a few isolated villages.

I watched one of the muleboys opening a tin of tuna with one of those old-fashioned can openers consisting of a sharp blade at right angles to a strange shaped 'shoulder' that acted as a point of leverage on the can. Actually he was making a bit of a hash of it and a bit of the oil inside was spilling out over the ground and over himself. In one of those dizzying moments of perfect recall, I saw once again my mother in the kitchen of our terraced house in Bromley Street, with a similar implement, expertly and swiftly opening a tin of Carnation condensed and sweetened milk. Less certainly but quite probably she was singing a song or teasing someone who had caught her eye. As likely she was telling some story.

In that strange state of being both, half way up a mountain and half a child again, I found myself slipping into my past and observing it at the same time. I was there and aware I was there, listening to her stories.

Perhaps it was hearing my compatriots reminisce and swap anecdotes but I realised that virtually all that I knew of my mother's side of the family I had constructed from her tales of her family and her childhood.

Her family, and background, the geography that shaped her world and therefore to an extent defined me and my brothers was therefore shaped by the stories she chose to tell us, or not to tell us.

She had been born into the poverty and struggles of Newcastle Upon Tyne during the depression years of the 1930s and settling with my father in the East Midlands, left the north east and an abusive relationship. Until I was sixteen she didn't go back. Her parents, a tough half-Irish shipbuilder William Dixon Lynam and his wife Evelyn had also left to find work in the south of England only to die within a year of each other when I was about five.

My mother's father was a Catholic who married a protestant

girl, a controversial thing in a city that still had Orange marches and competing senses of history. She was not brought up in the 'faith' and the local priest would turn up to persuade her mother and her daughters of the error of their ways. One day her father, returning back early from work, found his family in terrified tears being berated by the priest and threatened with hell and damnation. Picking him up by the collar he kicked him all the way down the stairs of the tenement building in which they lived. Later the priest snuck back and appeared in their doorway holding a big black book on an open page on which he had written the names of her mother, her sister and herself. Ostentatiously he took a pen and crossed out each of their names in deep blank ink and stalked off.

Despite this she remained remarkably tolerant of all people and ideas; only occasionally remarking that a church that demanded you had three fathers, your own, God and the local priest was in danger of overkill.

Her stories about her childhood were mixed up in an eclectic mosaic of childhood reminiscence, long-winded jokes, songs from the 30's and 40's – 'Mare's eat oats and Doe's eat oats' was a particular favourite I recall – fairy tales and on-the-spot improvisations. These were the stuff of long car journeys, bed time stories, an accompaniment to her baking as her young sons waited to lick the bowl.

Thus her childhood came woven in a fantastical tapestry of fact and fiction. Stories of dragons and demons were interwoven with vignettes of a lost world: of her standing as a little girl with her friends watching the dockers unload from the deep holders of the steamers, the stevedores joshing and teasing the kids but now and then tossing them the exotic gift of an orange or a liquorice root; of being thrown out of her house as a young girl and seeing her furniture piled up on the street; of her father keeping the family afloat during the hard times, making and mending cat's whisker radios, carving gravestones, reciting monologues and playing the harmonica in working men's clubs.

I fancifully wondered how and in what way all or any of this had contributed to me being more than half way up the highest mountain in North Africa? Ahead, Jonathan was reminiscing about a trip he had in the Australian Outback. I started to realise that we each were in a way working through our own personal script narrating why we were there and how it related to who we were. Some of us perhaps were experiencing an old story about an adventurous self lost perhaps in the noise of the school playground. Maybe the story was about proving something to someone who had long forgotten the mocking challenge they had laid down. Was an old cherished memory being replayed? Were we in a sense each climbing a different mountain played out through the stories we were prompted to tell.

But listening to them and observing my own rambling contributions I suddenly felt very cheery that we were all here to pay attention to each other. We may be climbing different mountains I mused, but we enjoy having each other to listen to our thoughts and so validate them.

This meditation was interrupted by Hugo's familiar cry of 'Let's crack on', and we all struggled back to our feet, clearing up the remainders of our stop and stumbled back onto the path. But as we measured our ascent in terms of a relentless Berber plod, the intriguing idea of a life defined by stories remained with me. To what degree were Marie, Hugo and Jonathan's tales about themselves or the *possibility* of themselves? And what was the difference anyway?

Towards the end of his life, Knulp explains how he came to be a tramp to his old friend the doctor. As a sexually adventurous school boy he had fallen under the spell of the passionate kisses of Franziska an ordinary girl with, for Knulp, extraordinary physical attraction. However she had denied him further delights as she could not be seen to be going out with a boy from the 'posh' school. Breaking his father's heart, an infatuated Knulp deliberately gets himself thrown out of the school and sent to a lesser institution where he finds himself in the same class as Franziska's brother. However he also finds that he is now more or less ignored by Franziska until one day he learns the terrible truth, discovering her, clothing in disarray, smoking a cigarette in the arms of the local mechanic.

Reading this, it appeared to me like a trivial tale of thwarted teenage lust seasoned with a little intellectual snobbery. But for Knulp it was a catastrophe, significant enough for him to explain the entire course of his existence in the last days of his life.

'Because you see – what can I say? – since then I've had good friends and casual friends, and even girl friends; but I've never relied on anyone's word and I've never given my own. Never again, I've lived my life as I saw fit, I've had my share of freedom and good things, but I've always been alone.'

Knulp feels compelled to give account of himself of the possibilities of his life as some sort of coherent narrative. Was Franziska the only reason he became a vagabond? Or was this the result of many other recognised and unrecognised events and impulses?

And as I grimly plodded upwards a thought crystallised that had been playing in the back of my mind for a few days. Knulp's story, had become enmeshed in mine years ago until it had become part of the narrative of who I was, even though I had hardly lived the facts of that story at all. Such is the power of story to engage and shape us. That a story about the wanderer free of obligation moving at the pace of a Berber plod had become essential to me.

At the summit we gazed at the breathtaking landscape of sunbroken rock and ice and snow that stretched all the way to the sea, slapped each other on the back, took photos and mentally tried to organise this chapter into the story of our lives and attempted to drink the miniature bottle of champagne that Abdu had thoughtfully provided.

Then, incongruously, Jonathan took a call from his bank manager. On the highest peak in North Africa, in the land of Leo Africanus the great wanderer, gazing west to the great Atlantic, someone wanted to talk to him about a Visa card.

The key being here in Morocco it seemed, was to accept that at any one time you were not dealing with reality per se but *a* reality, one of several possibilities, in which, at any moment the mundane could morph into the magical or the vice versa. It had happened in Sale, with 'Brahim and a now on the top of Toubkal. I wondered in the west why we find this so odd? Why so many people demand to see things one way only. Have we lost the 'tranquillity' to see this? If the magic ascent of Toubkal can transform into the mundanity of a bank manager's call, then surely back home the mundane and humdrum must in some way contain the possibility of magic?

And as I stood at the apex of a wrinkly curve of the planet, I smiled at the million ricochets of chance and improbability that make up the unique and accidental course of our lives. No wonder we need to be storytellers to stitch the random together and fulfil our need for purpose, for coherence, for meaning. Stories make sense of the choices we take. It is our account of who and why we are.

Stories are magic spells which we weave around the possibilities of our experience making things appear and disappear, connecting the unconnected, mysteriously rearranging the shape of circumstance and happenstance. Perhaps, for a while, they make who we really wanted or want to be disappear?

Powerful voodoo stuff.

But they are also the source of freedom and liberation. For at their best, stories and songs are also a way of playing with what might be. They are a form of experimentation in possibilities: possible futures, the possible present and the possible past. They allow us to inhabit next-to-worlds, they are way of being in an alternative more absorbing 'now', when the current moment traps and confines us. They are the way we understand ourselves and understand each other.

Telling stories about ourselves comes from a different place to the stories that are told to us. The stories which a community or society tells and repeats sometimes over generations. They are about shaping us, helping us to understand how to fit in. To an extent, 'Brahim's stories over the last few days had been about how the Berber people had seen themselves, what they wanted to have been. In the end, is our identity, formed less by the particular DNA of our birth and tribe and more by the stories that are told to us?

Many psychologists have noted the way stories shape us, providing role models that reconcile the paradoxes and tensions of living in a tribe or community in ways which are of course acceptable to the community as a whole. These are stories that show us how to be – perhaps even preparing us to be voluntary slaves.

Research by the psychologist David McClelland, indicated that those communities that contained children's stories that emphasised the need for high achievement also were correlated with high economic growth. Voluntary slaves at the coal face, the mill and the computer screen?

We write stories or we let them write us. They are a powerful medium whichever way the causation runs. Knulp's story made him the outsider, the Tanner's story led him to marry the girl who would betray him.

The descent was an unofficial breeze. We slid down most of Toubkal on our backsides through the snowfields. The trick is to grasp your ice axe, being prepared to use it as an emergency break, offer a silent prayer that the expanse of white and unsullied snow does not hide a large rock and let go, following 'Brahim over a slope as he shouts 'Scooby-Dooby Doo'.

There is nowhere that the wet, melting, slushy snow does not penetrate as you career down one improvised piste to another. If you dwelt on anything other than each succeeding microsecond of exhilaration then you would be overwhelmed with cold and intimations of incipient mortality.

Damp, elated, exhausted and ridiculously quickly we got to the refuge. For Marie and I, our separate personal stories of this adventure did not need to include another five hours hike back down to the Kasbah and we gratefully mounted Florence and another of the mules, to amble along in reflective and amiable conversation. Jonathan and Hugo were determined to walk all the way back.

The pass and path twisted and turned through remnant patches of snow, alongside torrential streams, the temperature rising and plunging as we moved from light to shade and back again. Fellow travellers were met rarely and perhaps it was this and a mixture of tiredness and thin air that led to me experience a lingering sense of enigma, woven with latent possibility as I swayed back and forward on Florence's back. I was haunted by the sudden powerful memory of my mother, the echoes and ghosts that this evoked. And I pondered the insight that stories possess the magic to weave our lives in so many different ways.

At the edge of my conscious awareness, next-to worlds and their possibilities skittered, watched and quietly giggled in the splutter of a stream or the slow ponderous meltdrop of a huge icicle. And wraith-like stories flitted amongst them, pale figures at the edge of the party waiting to be asked to dance.

As I shifted in on the broad woven saddle on the back of patient old Florence I found myself mourning for the infinity of untold stories we do not tell, afraid to embrace the possibilities that emerge from the random and surprising flow of events. A story told is one thing, a story lived another. No wonder they can make us nostalgic. The story we choose to tell of ourselves, *or is told for us*, intimately captures our relationship with the freedoms of being present and embracing possibility and the way we live our lives.

Eeeahhhruuu! One of the muleboys ran up behind Florence and gave her a large slap on the rump. She gave the abuse very little notice, perhaps there was a barely perceptible increase in pace.

'I guess reality does not include much in the way of possibilities for you?' I murmured scratching her ears.

'My story is not great,' said Florence as we plodded alongside a stream. 'But it is mine. And I have climbed mountains!'

'Well that is better than many,' I mused.

'But I could have been a racehorse, if my mother had made better choices, I could have been a contender!'

'You are riding with your mouth open,' Marie said ambling alongside.

'Actually I am having a conversation with Florence,' I said, 'who recognises the randomness of things and the need for stories to explain ourselves.'

'Really!?' said Marie.

'She's surprisingly wise.'

'For a mule,' muttered Florence.

I thought about my discoveries so far. First, that part of the art of life is to embrace the paradox and possibility of existence. Secondly, another facet of this art is to be able to rid ourselves for a sweet moment from the tyranny of our futures to discover and engage fully in the glorious rich possibility of the present.

I saw that the depth of our nostalgia was the extent to which we fail to do this. And that finally stories are the way we draw a personal line through the paradoxes and possibilities of our world, tying together the choices we have made and not made. Stories are often a balm to our disappointments and the pains of our nostalgia.

We rode on and as we passed under the walnut trees that cover the path up to the Kasbah, Florence slowed prompting another 'ehhrrrruuuuu', from one of the mule boys. I sensed a defiance as she slowed down even more. *'Involuntary slave she might be'*, I thought, *'but she still makes choices, a bit of her still belongs to herself.'* I leant forward to scratch her ears, did she move almost imperceptibly a bit faster?

I remembered a story from my childhood. It was called *Mister Dog* but I remember it as 'Crispin's Crispian, the dog who belonged to himself'. I must have asked my mother, and my father to read it to me a hundred times.

This was the story of a dog who welcomes the simple possibilities of life. He meets a fellow traveller, a boy who also belongs to himself and they open themselves to the steady unfolding of the day. And let things happen.

But what was it, I wondered, 'to belong to oneself'? It felt like there was a hidden truth here. To completely respond to the freedoms to be inconsistent and utterly present, would potentially be like engaging in a version of the rather wonderful but essentially self-destructive art of 'flipism', a life strategy in which you make all your decisions based upon the toss of a coin.

Such a life would be similar to the story of a psychiatrist named Luke Rhinehart in *The Dice Man*. Feeling bored and unfulfilled the hero of the book starts making decisions about what to do based on a roll of a dice. Within a few short pages the plot leads to dangerous sex, rape, murder, 'dice parties', and a tidal wave of confusion and disruption!

Notwithstanding the potential for a whole heap of trouble from such a lifestyle, it didn't seem much of a freedom to get nostalgic about anyway. To be free to be inconsistent and present seems to require something else to make it worthwhile.

Belonging to oneself? There must be freedom in that. And if anyone I had ever met had seemed to have the talent for belonging to themselves and evoking nostalgia in others it was my third representative; the wandering player, singer or musician. I had to hurry back to England. I was looking to spend time with a band of brothers and sisters with whom I judged myself to be a distant relative.

CHAPTER SIX

Saudade

Extraordinary how potent cheap music is
Noel Coward, Private Lives

London Road in Derby is not one of the world's great boulevards. To one side towers the chaotic mess of the old Derbyshire Royal Infirmary, capturing over 100 years of changing hospital architecture ranging from the Victorian brick paternalism through Maginot Line-inspired sixties concrete, to more recent this-and-that indecisiveness. On the other the teetotal plainly-dressed Central Methodist Hall stands disapprovingly amongst a range of take-away restaurants, pubs and bike shops. Amongst it all, almost incongruously are the Liversage Alms Houses built in the 19th Century from a bequest of a Derby tradesman who had lived during the reign of Henry VIII. Along the roadside, large weary Plane trees protect the passerby from the non-existent sun.

Yet I have affection for this place, it is part of my story and many roads have started from this one. I used to live just round the corner from here, in an old railway worker's cottage. And from here for two or more years I had made my music.

It was lunch time and I sat in a pub, which had been an old haunt, near the entrance to the hospital. I was killing an hour before catching the London train. Apart from me, the only life at the bar was an old man sitting reading a folded back copy of *The Sun*, a black and white mongrel dog curled up at his feet and two pretty young nurses giggling and sharing a packet of crisps. The bartender had disappeared after serving me my drink, leaving me wondering about a sandwich. The coloured lights from the fruit machine flickered mournfully. Outside it rained.

I gazed around the small bar. It had changed very little since I was in here more than twenty years ago. My friend Tim and I had played in this pub every Sunday night for over eighteen months. It was one of hundreds of gigs we played at the time.

The years span back as I gazed into the amber beer in my glass to the time when we belted out songs and ballads of love, lust and freedom. We juggled a trunk full of guitars, whistles, mandolins and flutes and Tim had played a fierce and furious fiddle that had the roll-necked purists tut, tut tutting and everyone else roaring their approval.

We were not so much on the bottom rung of the entertainment ladder, we used to joke, but still searching for the steps. We played in backroom bars, on the splintered floors where miners, railway workers and council workers met in frustrated camaraderie. We played to drown out the fruit machine, the musak and the earnest murmurings of hopeful young men and pale young girls.

I remember one night in a pub, not far from this one, playing to a packed bar. The room had old wooden beams holding up the floor above, so low you could reach up and touch them. The heat had made people's faces red and shiny as they stomped, clapped and cheered at Tim as he thundered through a Scottish reel called 'The De'il Amongst the Tailors', known to us as 'The Devil in Your Trousers'. Getting faster and faster till it was played at the pace of a runaway train, accompanied by me thrashing along on my guitar until eventually we juddered to halt and the place erupted. My guitar, after this mistreatment, was totally out of tune and I bent over struggling to hear it above the noise to return it to a passing relationship with decent pitch. As the B string remained stubbornly sharp I looked up as the applause, which has been gently subsiding, suddenly erupted again accompanied by laughter. Tim, with a mischievous look on his face, was balancing his fiddle bow vertically on his forefinger. I grinned to myself and went back my tuning. An instant later the crowd noise had stilled to a disbelieving murmur, there was a palpable sense of collective incredulity. I looked up. Tim had taken his finger away and there, as the slot machine uttered the odd electronic whimper, the fiddle bow floated, unaided in mid air, defying gravity and the laws of sense.

The pub clock tocked and time stopped.

And then a roar rose, primitive, guttural, sublime, a roar of outraged laughter, as Tim recovered the bow from hanging on the rusty old nail in the hidden in the gnarled timbers above his head and plunged into the next tune. Magic.

Smiling at this memory, I pondered the way that magic was a surprising quality of almost any passing moment in my search for the source of nostalgia. I don't mean conjuring, a sleight of hand, I mean it in the sense of calling a performance magical – something I believe Knulp would have understood. Magic happens when two or more realities co-exist in the same space and the one somehow connects to another, so that we sense something deeper perhaps 'alongside' is better – the 'next-to world'. This, I guess, does make the best conjuring in a sense magical. Magic is having one foot in this world and one in a possible world next to it. Conjurors are the Knulp-like figures who enable this.

It happened in here, in this bar I remembered. A tiny room with a red leatherette benches around the outside and three tables with some rickety wooden chairs. Less than twenty people could sit down comfortably, yet nearly ninety people had squeezed in one night to hear Tim and me play.

Our friend Nicci, was singing with us that night and her beautiful wistful version of the old Irish song 'The Sally Gardens' had reduced all of them to a still, and profound collective silence. It was the sort of silence in which people stare into the middle distance, seeing some half-remembered faces, recalling the soft murmured words of a stranger still to be met, a kind of exquisite regretfulness. It was the kind of moment when even big railway men with fists like shovels and humour like an old barber's razor get in touch with their feminine side.

I had found there is a Portugese word for it, which felt like a synonym of Knulp's nostalgia: saudade. It is a word that has no easy English translation but captures much of the notion of nostalgia. Wikipedia calls it: 'a vague and constant desire for something that does not and probably cannot exist … a turning towards the past or towards the future'. The word has been used to capture a sense of loss beyond sadness, for a homeland left forever, a husband lost at sea but it also can encompass the possibility of some hope, a wistful sense of a tomorrow, like two parted lovers who may, perchance, meet again. Saudade lies at the heart of many Portugese and Brazilian songs and it seemed an obvious lead in my search for Nostalgia as conjured by the strolling player.

And here I was in this portal to my past, having a beer, killing time waiting for a train. I was en route to London to meet an old friend I had not seen for several years and who would certainly have something to say about this phenomenon.

David was the obvious person to illuminate this part of my quest. He had spent a large part of his life in Brazil and was still in love with the place. Furthermore he was someone who unequivocally belongs to himself. He is a former international director of a large company marketing the brands that sit in our freezers, cupboards and bathrooms. But describing him as such completely fails to capture the high octane enthusiasm he brings to: raising an impossibly large family, playing boogie woogie piano, sitting on various committees of the great and the good, tramping through the corporate corridors as a roving trouble shooter and consultant.

He is possibly the most over-the-top, self-confident, self-assured person I have ever met. I had not seen him for years. I finished my beer and walked down to the railway station to get the London train to meet him.

'Do you know anything about saudade?' I had emailed him.

'Absolutely old boy,' he had replied. 'By the way it's usually plural, *saudades*, you can't relive emotions one at a time. You in London soon? Let's sink some caipirinhas and I'll tell you about it.'

Three hours later, a bar in London. He greeted me with his usual massive avuncularity.

'Hello old chap, good to see you!' he said laughing, thumping me on the shoulder with one hand whilst pumping my arm up and down with the other. 'Are things going well for you, completely gangbusters for me, completely gangbusters, still a couple of minutes in the wheel house before returning to man the pumps eh!' he said indicating two very large glasses containing ice, limes, and I suspected a fair amount of cane spirit.

With David, it is best to come straight to the point or run the risk of be shanghaied down some unexpected conversational tributary, so sitting down and letting him push a glass into my hand I began on my theme.

'I'm attempting to find out why so many people have this sense of a life not quite lived, a sort of world alongside, which they kind of mourn..."

'Ah! The road not taken!?' To the baffled amusement of those sitting around us he broke into song in what I presumed was Portugese.

'That,' he said, 'is one of the iconic songs from Bete Carvalho (probably called 'Saudades'). It's about a road that sings to Bete, and says he, (of course the road has to be male), has *saudades* for her, because he can remember when as a child, she ran on him with her barefeet. But now she walks on him with shoes. He feels they have lost touch. Has she been lost to a different world?'

'A more adult world?'

'Perhaps a more "constructed" world, more conventional, we

get trapped in our shoes sometimes, expected to walk in a particular way?'

'I remember as school boy,' I mused. 'The first thing I did at the start of the summer vacation was to take off my shoes and throw them away as they would be too small and worn for the start of the new term. Most of the summer I would walk around in bare feet. It used to drive my mother mad.'

'That's about it – the freedom to take off your shoes, get back in touch with the way of things, who you essentially are.'

'So *saudades*, mate, absolutely,' he went on. 'Lots of it in Brazil, it's in the DNA. The average Brazilian north and west of Rio is 33% rainforest Indian (and this area is probably 70 – 80% of Brazil's landmass). And this piece of DNA is the most intuitive and emotionally important part of the Brazilian character.

'It's a kind of intelligence you see, deeply intuitive. When travelling, we always followed the intuition of an Amazonian Indian because they could find the best restaurant, the best place to stay, the best path. Useful stuff. Even in an unknown terrain, they can draw in the sand where the next rivers are, and which way they are flowing. Nobody knows how they do this. So *saudades* also means "connected" with the natural world, the ebb and flow... Many Brazilians believe that everything is alive, and has a spirit – even insentient objects like sea, rocks, roads...Perhaps nostalgia happens when you get disconnected. You finished that one?'

I watched him wander over to the press around the bar and immediately engage the couple to his right in conversation. I quite liked the notion that nostalgia might reflect a kind of intelligence, a way of discerning half-hidden things and our sense that we lack the freedom to reconnect.

When he returned the conversation naturally flowed onwards to the demise of his classic Jaguar sports car, how he was going to save the ice cream industry from melt down; the eclectic adventures of his family but later, as I wandered back to my hotel, full of South American steak, several caipirinhas and beer, I was really struck by this idea of 'connection', that the magic of music and song connects us not just to memories but also to possibilities that have, do and will exist for us. I wondered at the power of the singer and the song to do this.

Perhaps music induces a kind of trance, in which new perspectives and truths can emerge – other worlds can suggest themselves and get heard. We are connected or reconnected to the world that could have been and the world that is trying to reveal itself. In it there has to be complicity – a collusion between performer and audience to suspend the rules of belief, or convention, or expectation. This is freedom as a quiet act of revolution.

Is that Knulp's gift – the singer, the musician and the storyteller? To weave a spell that casts a collective trance and in which we revolt against our chains? It is powerful stuff. The travelling storyteller, the strolling player, and the wandering minstrel have a long history in most cultures. In India and Morocco and many other places there is still is a role for the storyteller standing at the village well or in the market place, telling a tale that may be hundreds, if not a thousand years old. They fall in and out of favour. Their power has always been recognised as dangerous – people in power don't want the people they control put into a trance and have 'possibilities' put into their minds – the voluntary slaves are not to be provoked lest we become less compliant. (In Europe in the Middle Ages the minstrel and his bawdy songs were replaced by Troubadors, junior aristocrats, so much more refined).

They are outsiders, sometimes regarded as little more than scoundrels, other times like O'Carolan, the Irish harper, figures who are respected and even revered. They are not members of a society or community but on the edge of it choosing but also being encouraged, to move on. But they are given a special privilege; for within the trance they conjure, they are able to say the unsayable, point to another reality, highlight the contradictions that others would sweep out of sight. The clown uses the magic of joke to say things that otherwise would offend or provoke or at least to render that offense or provocation unactionable. The fool in *King Lear* is but one in a long line of singers, satirists, storytellers who first weave a trance and then say the unsayable:

King Lear: *Does though call me a fool boy?*
Fool: *All thy other titles thou hast given away; that thou wast born with.*

The dissenters, lacking the opportunity to create the magic that protects the truthsaying, would not have been so free. The storyteller and the singer can also find themselves in trouble when they forget this.

Around the start of the second Gulf War, the American, all girl country group, the Dixie Chicks performed in concert at the Shepherd's Bush Empire theatre in England. During the introduction to their song 'Travelin' Soldier', the Texan, Natalie Maines, said: *'Just so you know, we're on the good side with y'all. We do not want this war, this violence, and we're ashamed that the President of the United States is from Texas.'*

Wrapped in a tune and a song people might not have noticed. But as a statement from a stage this did not play well in the USA. Right wing shock jocks fulminated against them, their cds were burned in the streets; radio stations stopped playing their music; they were denounced, reviled and threatened. They refused to be cowed and released a song called 'Not Ready to Make Nice'– a song of defiance and challenge.

And for many people they remain unforgiven.

Telling your truth is a risky business. No wonder we are so often afraid to do so. Walking along the streets of London, it began to rain, in that misty, seeping insidious sort of way that marks southern rain from the brusque stair rod variety found in the north of England. Suddenly I felt sad. Alcohol is the father of melancholia and a city in the dark and the rain, the mother. There are ghosts in this town for me and I found them walking alongside me. It can often be like this in this Dickensian city. Each of them turns up, like a lover lost and you stare back into the shadowy lands of memory trying to recognise the path that took you away from them. Or they away from you. And you realise, in their reproachful gaze, that in the parting, a bit of who you really were, was disconnected.

The singer and the street. Turning my collar to the cold, I shook my head to rid myself this remembrance – is connection always bitter-sweet? Is that why the term 'nostalgic' is so apposite? *Saudades.*

From somewhere down a gloomy alley came the sound of an infectious inane song inviting me to shake my body. For a moment my mood lightened and I smiled at my fickle despair. '*Ah, how extraordinary how potent cheap music is*', I quoted Noel Coward to myself. This train of thought continued as reaching one of the seedy, over-priced hotels in which London shelters its many visitors, I ended up sitting on my bed, bottle of beer in hand, watching the neon lights play on the wall, listening to the endless traffic rumble past and trying to ignore the unpleasant looking stain on the carpet.

I sensed Knulp opposite me in the shadows.

'You were a storyteller and player Knulp. What was in the magic you made?' Knulp was silent for a moment.

'I don't know, a kind of unshackling?'

'From what?'

'From other people's stories,' he wondered, 'so we can connect to how the world might be, so we can re-imagine our own story?'

'The great story tellers and singers connect to us when we

recognise they are telling our truth,' I proposed. 'And when we feel nostalgic, we recognise we are not living ours.'

'Something that would feel more authentic?' said Knulp.

Authentic! Now that, I thought, is a provocative word. It comes from the Latin – *autos* 'self' and *hentes* meaning 'doer, being'. As I turned the bottle around in my hand holding it so that my chin rested on the opening, I wondered if that was it. Was it all about becoming connected to the real us?

What is it to be authentic? Life, if it is a paradoxical flow of possibilities, is therefore also a flow of decision making. On what basis do we take these decisions? On the basis of the maintaining a consistent narrative to our lives or on the basis of something deeper and braver, that which feels truer to ourselves.

For a glorious, inebriate moment it all fell into place. Firstly, a nostalgia for freedom arises in us, most when we sense, with childlike uninhibited clarity, the world of paradox and potential. Secondly, it grows in that moment, when as voluntary slaves, we realise we have surrendered ourselves to a limited life, tyrannised by fears of future consequence and circumscribed by the obligation of appearing consistent, trapped in a story much of which someone else has written. And from these two, seeing ourselves mired in the sticky swamp of procrastination, inauthentic and limited, it mourns our disconnection from some deeper sense of ourselves.

And, as outside a couple giggled and stumbled down the corridor and started knocking on someone else's door, it appeared, complete, perfect and profound. The secret revealed in the now, in our absorption in the potential world, is not nostalgia for who we could have been as much as who we might be; the 'who' through all our travails is trying to emerge at this moment. And below the shifting, changing shape of our narrative and personality is the evolving truth of our identity. Who we are, our search for identity, is a call from the future more than a cry from the past; it is about who we are becoming rather than who we have been, although we may interpret it as such. It is about living a truer story. It is the fidelity of people like 'Brahim.

The possibilities we sense around us, are the opportunities for experiments in who we might be, our nostalgia is for those Baboushka-like moments when our own self came knocking and we did not let him or her in.

And as I looked in the gloom past the ghosts sitting on my bed I came to the point of certainty – that I was, we were, not fixed, a 'real self' to be discovered but an evolving self to a destination that exists but cannot be reached. And so, responding to the possibilities of the world around us, our mission should be to travel well. And yet this makes us fearful and makes the societies we live in anxious to curb this dynamic, to retain cohesiveness.

Perhaps I thought, opening another bottle of beer, the next stage of our evolution doesn't have to always gradually emerge, sometimes it occurs in a blinding, obvious moment of truth. I remembered why I first fell in love with the possibility of rock music. I had a friend at school, Adrian. He was a quiet bespectacled fellow. Kind of intense. Not one of guys who felt that moderate sporting prowess gave them an excuse to strut. He had a friend called Kevin and another called Paul and together with some other guy they had a band. I'd never really heard them play, I wasn't into rock music at the time, being a trumpeter, but someone told me they were quite good. They were playing a gig at our local school fair and I wandered over the night before to hear them rehearse. They were playing in a big empty classroom with a low stage. At the back Kevin sat behind a silver drum kit, the bass player was looking intently at a piece of paper stuck to a mike stand. Paul sat nonchalantly on the edge stage strumming some chords. Adrian stood to my left, playing a gorgeous sunburst Commodore semi-acoustic guitar, a serene look on his face. They were playing a guitar instrumental which, despite the hesitant bass playing, sounded mournful and beautiful. I was transfixed.

They nodded their heads to me in that half-acknowledging male adolescent way when they finished.

'What's that tune called?' I asked.

'Instrumental Number 2,' muttered Paul.

'Why's that?' I asked.

'Because it's the second one,' he replied. He considered the end of his guitar and adjusted a machine head. 'And, well, we haven't even got a name for the first one yet, it being Instrumental Number 1.'

'Who wrote it?' I asked.

'I guess we did.'

I think it was one of the most astonishing statements I had heard in my life to date. Up to that point, writing a song or a piece of music, was something I thought only a real expert did, carefully drawing out complex symbols and marks on manuscript paper – a mysterious task that I had always felt was completely beyond me. And here they were, just making up songs! I knew Paul could read music a bit, but I was sure Adrian couldn't. It had never occurred to me that you didn't need to write down songs to write them, a good memory or a little cassette player would suffice.

At that moment, who I was took a huge leap to somewhere new. It was a tipping point in my life – a great experiment in authenticity. I bought a guitar, naturally a red sun-burst Commodore semi-acoustic, and started to play, strumming out the simple chord patterns in the Beatles 'made easy' book. After that I didn't learn other people's songs much, preferring to write my own: poor, inadequate, derivative though they might be, they were honest expressions of who I felt I was. This was change for me that went beyond mimicry, it connected me to who I was becoming and gave it form. Yes I could trace a line back to the little boy, holding his mother's hand, watching barges, but it was more than that. Being able to write songs, create music, perform, entertain, shaped me, engaging me for years in a journey of exploration.

Perhaps these essential moments come rarely, perhaps they are always there but we don't see them. But they are there waiting to redefine us. They are invitations to revolution. At that drunken moment I could not imagine anything more sad than this failure to connect.

I raised a toast to all my ghostly companions. The freedom to be inconsistent, and the freedom to be present are both servants of our ultimate freedom which is to let our identities evolve authentically. The bitter sweet melody evokes in us that bit of us that we have not let grow. The songwriter's words provoke suppressed memories and insights into who we wanted and are still trying to be.

CHAPTER SEVEN

The Tiger in the Cage

*It's the hole in each ear
That lets in the fear,
That, and the absence of light!*

Spike Milligan, Bump

I had, perhaps not for the first time, woken sitting on top of the bedclothes, still semi-dressed, head on chin and a terrible ache in my shoulders. Starting to circulate, were the rumours of an incipient pain in my temples. A cold grey light slouched in from a dirty window, unhidden by the curtains I had failed to close.

Glaring at me, a woman, dark hair framing a severe expression and wearing a monogrammed pink overall was standing at the foot of my bed. She was holding two small bottles of shampoo.

'I make up the room?' she demanded in an East European accent.

'No thanks,' I muttered. She looked at me with a kind of baleful disgust.

'Do you want these?' she said pushing the mini shampoos towards me. 'Cleaning?'

'No thanks, I am fine,' I croaked.

She gave me a final look of contempt and marched out. Pulling the door closed behind her with a thump, I heard her lapse into another language born of the European plains, volubly explaining, no doubt to a colleague, about the wretch she had just encountered.

Wearily and gingerly I pulled myself into a vertical position and went over to the window to look out and see what the day might offer. The view was of another brick wall scarcely more than an arm's length away. Just below me was the purple and grey snout of an air conditioning unit. Given the intense heat in the room it was clearly not working. Vainly I tried to open the window. It was painted shut.

'Life in a central London 4 star hotel,' I muttered to myself. 'What time is it?'

According to my phone, it was 6.45 am. *'Bloody hell!'* I thought. I considered completing the guest questionnaire placed conveniently next to my bed. A diatribe about overpriced London hotels, inconsiderate maids and deliberate suffocation momentarily appealed but I dismissed the idea figuring any reply would be filed under 'land fill'.

I filled the little plastic kettle in the bathroom and sat on the edge of the bed waiting for it to boil and trying to recapture the exhilaration of the previous night. But I know only too well what the cold light of dawn does to last night's great ideas. And so it was with this one. Last night I had, I felt, discovered a universal truth, this morning it was a half-baked egg. I thought I had answered the question of what nostalgia was – our inability to let ourselves be who we might evolve to be, but I had only answered half the question.

Morosely, I realised the bigger question was why did we let this happen? Why did we not take the more adventurous path, why did we not embrace possibility and the individual inconsistency that must arise, why did we turn away from the person that we might become? Why did we let ourselves become nostalgic, and Knulp provoke us so? Bollocks!

My friend Jason Webster would say simply it was fear. He wrote in his lovely book *Duende*: *'We often end up doing what we almost want to do because we lack the courage to do what we really want to do'*. He, at first, ended up living in Italy because he wanted to live in Spain. Perhaps we were just afraid of uncertainty. Perhaps we were afraid of consequences – the disapproval or hurt of others?

The kettle boiled and I tore open one of the little sachets of coffee, spilling irritating amounts of rough brown gritty granules across the table top. Then the effort of releasing the milk from its little container dropped fatty globules of milk next to the spilt coffee.

'Oh piss off world.' I surrendered and lay back on the bed, resting my head on the wilful refusal of the pillow and dropped into a bad-tempered doze.

Coming round a while later, I decided the odds for the best coffee were to be found in nearby Covent Garden, and so splashing a little water on my face, I took a stroll round and found a decent café and sat down with an Americano and a glass of water.

Savouring the sharp bitter taste of the coffee, I sat there and thought about this issue: the nearly rather than the really. I enjoy thinking when I am grumpy, it soothes the soul.

'*So reviewing the situation,*' I thought, '*nostalgia arises when we deny ourselves three freedoms, most of all the freedom to express the evolving sense of who we are. And how and why do we do that, is the new question,*' I noted.

Cue another hesitant sip of coffee and a mental summoning of Knulp who remained elusive.

'*So is it fear?*' I wondered therefore to myself. '*Or even cowardice?*'

Certainly this has been, probably since time immemorial, the contemptuous accusation of the rebel and would-be rebel against the conventional and the narrow; the restrained, cautious existence of the suburban idyll. Not many writers celebrate the delights of suburbia; it's not cool to come from the prim and proper petit bourgeoisie; the adventurer and the revolutionary rarely aspire, as we say in Derbyshire, to be 'steady'.

Risk and reward are close bedfellows. Often the more rewarding option is accompanied by a more serious downside. For the original slaves the option to become a Renegado would have had some serious risks. First of all, it would have been the fear of never seeing your family again, your home town, your local football team. Secondly, I guess the threat of being burned alive in a cobbled square in front of a crowd of souvenir seeking onlookers would have been off-putting. Certainly it was the fear of damnation, inculcated into all by an obedience-seeking church. Someone once told me that religion was a very good way of controlling very large numbers of people – you are always on God's radar.

Yes I guess, perceiving the potential downside of choosing the richer alternative – separation, an unpleasant death, eternal damnation and never seeing your side play a home game – would put most people off straying from the straight and narrow path. Obviously then most of us would seek a less threatening, easier life.

Are we too frightened then to become modern Renegadoes, taking the more rewarding but more uncertain option when it arises? When the road beckons, when the more radical opportunity offers itself, do we collude with society to deliberately create a scenario full of painful consequences such that, if we don't take the conservative path and stick to the straight and narrow, horrible things will happen? Is our willing search for a 'mortgage', for example, and its hideous half-sister the secured loan, simply a collusive piece of social engineering designed to cow and frighten us into fearful submission? The mortgage: a wonderful piece of voluntary enslavement in which the slave takes all the risk and pays handsomely for it! Are we so feeble? I put this sudden mental outburst down to caffeine plus background grumpiness.

Yet you might argue that history is full of people who would accept the risk of these terrible consequences. Down the road from this café was Tyburn, London's favourite spot for public execution. Here, alongside the miscreants, cutpurses and hoodlums who suffered an ignoble death, also expired those, who in matters of faith, conviction and inspiration, believed they were on a path to a richer life. But these are the people who get written about, become remembered, leaving plagues, signs and the odd eponymous tea shop.

Most of us, however, are the unwritten members of history – the ones who in several little ways each day betray our desires, our convictions and ourselves. We are the ones who take the safer, conservative, more predictable options. Yet, and yet, we seem to remember that a piece of who we are lies in the opportunities from which we have turned away. Ironically, that which we fear most is often that which we desire most, it feels truer to who we are. It is not that the option is richer just because it is denied but because the option *is* risky and therefore exciting.

My old friend, the psychologist Michael Apter, calls this point of maximum uncertainty and excitement the 'dangerous edge', beyond which lies trauma. Without the 'threat' of trauma, he observed, paradoxically there would be no excitement. If a fairground ride didn't go very high or very fast, travelling on it for many wouldn't be very rewarding.

The truth is we all like doing risky things but don't always feel able to do the risky things that we particularly like. These are the 'if only options'. If only: I was older, richer, younger, didn't have kids, had less responsibility, hadn't married *him*!

But not many of us are full time paid up voluntary slaves. All of us sometime, somewhere will take the riskier option. We are naturally audacious – sometimes. Audacious is a word I like. It captures the idea of both risk taking and rule breaking. It is tempting to think of people as either risk takers or risk avoiders but thinking of the acquaintances, friends and companions that are the menagerie of my social life, would I happily class any them as wholly one or the other? I think not. I myself am a nervous passenger, don't like standing on the edge of tall buildings and find some sorts of personality very intimidating, yet fly micro-lights, have in my youth climbed out of the window of a moving car and back in through the opposite one and quite happily taken over compering a music festival when the official MC fell over drunk.

If we are capable of being both audacious rebels and cautious 'voluntary slaves', then what shapes our decision to march towards the 'edge' of opportunity or retreat from it?

'It's like a tiger and a cage,' Mike once told me. 'Put the tiger in the cage and it's exciting, separate the tiger from the cage and you run for your life!'

Some of us can put a psychological cage around the riskier more rebellious opportunities we face and embrace them. Mike calls this a 'protective frame'. Perversely, is it a lack of cages that makes so many of us voluntary slaves?

I watched a be-helmeted cyclist picking his way through the burgeoning early morning traffic – I wondered if he realised this was far more dangerous than swimming in shark infested waters, flying a stunt aircraft or gluing your fingers together with super glue. The thing is, I thought, what is dangerous, what requires audacity, is very much what we perceived to be so.

The more I thought about it the more clearly I could see that for many of us, the richer option – perhaps doing what we really want to do – comes associated with a possibly traumatic effect. Not necessarily physical trauma – there seem to be a whole load of potential social traumas pushing us in the direction of voluntary slavery. They range from social disapproval, embarrassment, rejection, scape-goating, ostracisation, abuse, to more tangible things like divorce and redundancy.

As the humanity of London started to swirl around me, the thing that struck me was that these were things that threatened to put us on the outside of a community. We do seem to have enormous fear of this. Evolutionary psychologists argue that we are adapted to be animals that fit in, so perhaps the perceived power of these threats to help us to be more collaborative, cohesive and as we have seen *consistent,* fulfils an important social process creating strong communities which in turn can protect us as individuals. But, I wondered, as the cyclist cut up that most fearsome of traffic beasts, a red London bus, why, despite all these apparent threats, can some people maintain a protective frame and approach their dangerous edge.

I mentally wandered back to another coffee and another trip to Morocco: To Fez and the Clock Café in the Medina. Situated deep in the medieval city inside a few hundred years of domestic history, it is a meeting place of people, personalities and cultures. In its middle is the typical courtyard around which stand the four internal sides of the Clock Café. Suspended by thin wires in mid air North African instruments hang floating above the hub-bub. On little tables rising through the several stories you may find young Moroccan performers, travelling westerners, artists, tourists and ex-pats meeting to exchange stories, drinking coffee, learning belly-dancing, calligraphy, drumming.

The place was created by a guy called Mike Richardson. Mike looks a bit like a postgraduate IT boffin, red-haired, tall, slim, jeans and wire spectacles. But a particularly ebullient one, fizzing with energy and charm, which was probably what lay behind his success as the Maitre d' of two of London's most prestigious restaurants – The Ivy and the Wolseley.

I remembered having a coffee with Mike on the roof terrace of the Café. To me the 'why' of what he'd chosen to do seemed obvious – having dropped in the previous evening and sidled past a mature western woman energetically belly-dancing in a North Face jacket to the driving rhythms of some Moroccan percussionists – I could see the place was a crossroads for the surprising and delightful. But how, I had wondered did you get from the status, security and dependability of a career in the top restaurants of London and New York to serving camel burgers and non-alcoholic beer in Fez?

For Mike there was an accidental and intuitive vein to the story. He had been trying to purchase a restaurant in Istanbul, failed, someone suggested Fez, and he decided this was the place almost immediately. However he was frustrated by the process of property purchase in Morocco itself and after failing to buy several places, he took to carrying a plastic bag full of money around Fez in the hope of adding some velocity to the purchasing process. But how, I asked him, what is it about him that meant he could do this?

'I guess you've got to know what you want in yourself,' he said. 'You've got to be certain about what it is that matters for you.' He went on, 'And you've got to be prepared to change and adapt until it feels right.'

Thinking about it, he was tapping into two freedoms – being experimental and inconsistent about how things might be, and strong and focused on how this must all relate to the person he was trying to become. Tellingly he added, 'I'm not here to change the world, I'm here to make my world.'

Is this how you build a protective frame and approach your 'dangerous edge'? By focusing on your strengths – the things that both define who you are and that you feel good at – and by allowing yourself the freedom to experiment and change your mind. Not about the core of who you are, but how that might be expressed?

Back in Sale I had repeatedly glimpsed the essential paradox of our existence: that we need to both rebel and fit in, be a slave and a Corsair and there is always a price to pay for choosing one too much above the other. And over the last few days I had come to recognise that we are often encouraged by subtle and not so subtle means to follow the well worn path. Being the rebel is often dangerous, being inconsistent is socially problematic.

But is avoiding trauma and threat the whole of the story of voluntary slavery? What are the rewards of voluntary slavery? Are they greater than purely an absence of fear? My thoughts turned back to my guide, Knulp, and the people he met on his wanderings.

It would be easy to argue that Knulp's friends, burdened by the obligations and responsibilities of family were enslaved by caution – but Knulp did not despise them, often encouraging them to recognise the value they had created in their lives, and in his moment of despair seemed to regret he had not done the same.

Perhaps they had forsaken the ability to see the possibilities and next-to worlds that surrounded them, perhaps weighed down by the need to take care of the future they had lost the ability to be as actively engaged in the present. Perhaps they had even surrendered the richness and paradox of their own identities and the path that this might lead them on. But Knulp saw they had *something*.

In a very touching scene with Schlotterbeck the tailor, once destined for greater things but now living in poverty with an overlarge family and a mountain of worries, Knulp tells him about his own son who cannot know that he, Knulp the wanderer, exists. We both pay a price he seems to be saying.

In the old Medina in Fez, after my chat with Mike Richardson, I saw signs of the potential in conforming and accepting consistency. The Medina had hardly changed in hundreds of years. I sat under the awning of a local café by the Bab Boujloud gate gazing at a scene that would be more or less completely recognisable to the greatest wanderers of Morocco, Leo Africanus – a refugee from the expulsion of the Moors from Granada who lived in Fez, and trekked through North Africa and Italy – and Ibn Battuta. Ibn Battuta, the greatest of all wanderers, who travelled over 30,000 miles in his life, set out from Fez on one of his incredible journeys in the autumn of 1351. Crossing the Atlas Mountains he journeyed for eight or nine days to a town called Sijilmasa on the oasis of Tafilalt, waited there for the winter season to begin, before leaving as part of an enormous camel train to cross the vast Sahara. As he packed his bags, he and I would have gazed upon virtually the same changeless scene.

Yet most people stayed.

Within the Medina.

Within the web of narrow streets, partially covered for shade, were contained, tiny boutiques built into walls, each retailing the different necessities of domestic history. Here a man sits on a raised platform with a pile of timber and sharp tools all around his precarious position, making little cedar buckets probably for the hamman.

In the shadows, butchers stand in little open-faced shops the size of broom cupboards behind stone slabs offering piles of offal, goats heads, cows feet, stomachs and other entrails, as well as more western friendly joints and sausages. A fresh decapitated camel's head stuck on a spike makes clear in one what is on offer.

On another stall, a mournful but unprotesting chicken sits on a weighing scale whilst the shopkeeper and a lady in a light blue djellabah with a white head scarf, negotiate over the price and weight. With a mutual nod of the head, the chicken is dispatched in the time it takes for the shopkeeper to turn from the scales to the block.

In one dark corner, I nearly trip over an ancient woman, squatting against a wall, selling big juicy snails from a yellow plastic bucket. Along the strip are shoe shiners and two types of beggar; the pleader, eyes rolling and palms lifted, and the silent, resigned, almost catatonic; guarded by a tin cup. The smell of heat and humanity is seasoned by mint tea, cumin and further along, the stink from the tanneries.

There is an incessant integrated movement of people up and down these streets, performing a natural wave-like snakedance, as people pushing hand carts move to supply the haberdasher, ironmonger and apothecary. One in particular, laden with bags of cement, careers down the slight incline to the Qaraouiynine Mosque, one guy grimly hanging on the back whilst his fellows scamper down beside him laughing and chattering.

Across the square, people and mules move through the centuries. The mules on spindly legs carrying enormous loads of russet coloured cans of gas, piles of sheepskins and water bottles. People engage with each other.

And, from my vantage point of a London morning, I notice they seem content. A modern Moroccan woman in an elegant Italian suit sways past followed by women deep in conversation, waddling along in djellabahs and head scarves. Men dress in jumpers, baseball caps, more traditional costumes. Skins are coloured like old Cedar, some containing a map of the world in roads and rivers. Men walk hand in hand with men, women with women. Cheeks brush cheeks and backs are slapped.

How is this? History here does not seem about revolution just a gentle morphing. Where is the restlessness to change? Where are the people who don't accept the status quo, and stimulate movement? Many of the Medina live in poverty but they do not seem to live in fear. Is there a questioning about the lot with which those of the Medina have been cast?

And back there is Fez. Sitting at a table in the company of men and cigarette smoke, was I amongst voluntary slaves? Beneath the bustle and noise, people were essentially conventional, conforming, dutiful. Religion and community seemed to structure and order their lives. But there was more than fear here. But what was it?

CHAPTER EIGHT

The Pleasures of Slavery

Deliverance for me is not in renunciation, I feel the embrace of freedom in a thousand bonds of delight ...

Rabindranath Tagore, *Gitanjali*

God, I love Hong Kong! I have been coming here since before 1997, when a wet and corpulent Governor General took down the British flag and went home in the rain. In a world in which millions now routinely travel widely, it remains a special destination. I found myself there again a few weeks after my trip down to London in search of saudade, the essence of nostalgia and the next question that it raised: why we don't follow the adventurous road that opens up before us?

My being in Hong Kong was another piece of the serendipity that on good days carries me along and shapes my life. I was here for a useful, paid-for purpose, but I instinctively knew that this would be a good place to be for my more esoteric quest. The direct result of *realpolitik*, colonial aspiration, dirty dealings and the Midas dance of trade, I had great faith in the deep and inherent absurdity and possibility of this place to shine some more light on my musings.

Perhaps it is because of its mongrel accidental background – Queen Victoria was *not* amused to find herself monarch of a small, rather disreputable island in the South China Sea – but life seems distilled to its essence in Hong Kong. More money is gambled on the last night of the racing season at the Happy Valley racecourse than on the whole of the UK flat racing season. There are more skyscrapers than New York. On Sunday morning thousands of Phillipino maids sit on rugs and cushions, surrounded by huge homebound parcels, chattering away in the shade of the atrium of HSBC tower, the shrill voices, sounding like an aviary of particularly raucous birds. In the street market just beyond Mandarin Oriental Hotel and the smooth Chinese chic of Shanghai Tang on Peddar Street, I have wandered in the steamy heat through stalls of linen, plastic pots, fish, hens and watched a portly Chinese lady, shrieking in frustration, chase a large eel down the street.

It is the notion of next-to-worlds actualised. The hermetically-sealed deodorised brand emporiums of the Harbour Shopping Plaza where people pay inscrutable amounts for a Louis Vuitton handbag is just a short ride on the MTR to the raucous, smelly cacophony of the Ladies Market in the heart of the Mong Kok District where a more than fair copy of the same thing can be purchased for a few dollars.

Jan Morris describes a scene that seems quintessential. Watching the unloading of live pigs from the mainland, cruelly imprisoned in wire cages which cut and torment them, then being transported on wheelbarrows squealing in terror to the slaughter house, she saw: '… *a line of small girls in almost exaggeratedly English uniforms […] demure and dimpled they filed past, their faces exuding school pride and team spirit: and they took not the slightest bit of notice as they walked daintily by, of the doomed animals screaming in their torture chambers.*'

Past, present, east, west, the profane and the sacred and spiritual, the commonplace with the magical, a hundred years of British rule left trams, double-decker buses and hardly any taxi drivers speaking English. And in this cocktail of diversity arises, not the near-anarchic exuberance of a Rio or Mumbai but the careful, diligent order of Hong Kong. It is not that Hong Kong Chinese are grey or boring, anyone who has been to a Chinese market or festival will know this is not true, but stereotypically they are dutiful, reserved and very aware of social position. They are the masters of the fitting-in world. Culturally and traditionally, Hong Kong Chinese respect the position not the person, and therefore no matter how hopeless the incumbent, deference will out.

This must be a fundamental feature of voluntary slavery. Every time we let ourselves be directed by someone who we follow because of their position rather than their worth; when we speak someone else's mind rather than our own then we have committed a small act of treason against ourselves and nostalgia is our penance. But my search was now not for what happens but why we let it.

Some of the more obvious benefits of voluntary slavery had been reinforced by my journey out here. The company paying for me to fly out to Hong Kong had kindly booked a business class ticket on the Friday night British Airways flight out of Heathrow. Much to my childlike delight, pressure of sales had resulted in being upgraded to first class for the twelve hour plus journey.

And so I had found myself sitting in the airship-like first class cabin at the front of a 747, cross-legged on the enormous single seat, carefully angled towards the aircraft windows listening to an orchestral version of *You Only Live Twice* on my perfectly engineered head phones. As I sipped a glass of Krug champagne, we banked over the River Thames and the evening sunlight danced in shifting patterns around my private space.

I have always loved the flight out to Hong Kong and this was one of the most memorable. After the sweet attentions at dinner of a rather matronly stewardess and a fantastically obsequious purser and then a long night's sleep involving fresh linen and feather pillows, I awoke to find the plane was flying on an unbelievably clear day along a seemingly endless archipelago of green islands in the South China Sea. The sense of being in a graceful airship was reinforced, not only because of the cabin being so quiet as the engines are far behind, but also that you can easily see out of the windows on both sides – the size of it being no more than the lounge of a decent sized house in Tunbridge Wells. We seemed to drift in a kind of airborne reverie for what seemed like hours over an Eden-like vista of the bluest sea and verdant, pendant drop isles.

Over breakfast of scrambled egg and champagne, I came to the not so astounding conclusion that voluntary slavery, or fitting in, could be driven by much more than an absence of fear!

I was staying in a hotel I knew as the Great Eagle on Peking Road, although it is now called the Langham. It's not actually on Hong Kong island but a short distance across the harbour in Kowloon. As soon as I arrived, I hastily dumped my suitcase in my room and headed out again into the late afternoon sunshine. It has been my custom to head off on a long walk as soon as I arrive in Hong Kong. My body is usually registering a time of day that demands coffee and the early morning papers, and my personal theory is exposure to the sun's altitude and direction resets the body clock. I headed down to the Star Ferry pier. I kept my eyes resolutely ahead as sub-continent tailor after sub-continent tailor thrust leaflets in my hand.

It was an oft repeated route, across to Central on Hong Kong island, up around back streets past the old church on the way up to Peak Railway back down along the waterfront a little way, a ferry back over to Kowloon and the along the water front, the modern esplanade around Tsim Cha Sui past the Arts Centre and the Space Centre. These have always seemed to be anachronistic virility symbols set on reclaimed land that was once the terminus of possibly the greatest railway line of them all: the Trans-Siberian Railway. The great Peninsular Hotel, still waiting patiently for long-gone intrepid passengers who have made their way overland from Russia by steam train, or stepped ashore from the first class cabin of the RMS Carthage of the Peninsular and Oriental Steam Navigation Company, gazes a little sadly on these modernist edifices and their *parvenu* inhabitants. Still it keeps itself well enough on the nouveau-riche arriving by limousine from the new airport.

By now it was twilight and as darkness rapidly grew I turned away from the smooth, modern westernised, sterilised, aspiration of elegance to the cacophony and chaos of back street Tsim Sha Tsui. It always feels like vertigo this moment as you tumble from one world to the next. Into a mêlée of lights, the sweet stink of damp heat, humanity and street food; from the sophistication of the waterfront to this tarantella of urgent activity: massage parlours, electrical shops, food stalls, haberdashers, drapers, boutiques and restaurants from the far corners of Asia.

Pausing on a street corner as a long black Mercedes pushed its way through the common press, I looked up at the buildings, dirty, dark and mean, an anonymous unknown behind a neon supernova and wondered at who lived and watched from the blank spaces rarely lit by a light from within. Were these just the windows of shabby offices importing trinkets and cottons from places such as Pakistan – or did people live there?

Away from the gaudy flames for the tourist moths, Honk Kong has serious levels of poverty and a level of homelessness that sees hundreds of thousands of people literally living in cages. Constructed by dividing up small apartments of around sixty-five square metres with wood and wire partitions, up to eighteen people can live with all their possessions, one on top of another.

And yet Hong Kong has remarkably low levels of crime, particularly violent crime. What is it about the Chinese, I wondered, that means they can endure such a brutal counterpoint between the shopping cathedral of the Harbour Shopping Plaza and the next-to world of back street Tsim Sha Tsui?

There must be very little pleasure and not much that's voluntary about survival here if you were not one of the wealthy and well-heeled, undertaking a little ethnic shopping.

I picked my way through the crowds of young affluent Chinese, tourists and the dispossessed, past the booming of the HMV store. Walking through the streets as a single, white male is to run the gauntlet of insistent questioning, some direct, some muttered from the side of the mouth as eyes glance restlessly around: 'Fake watch sir, Rolex?', 'Come here, good time!', 'Suit? Glasses? Good time, good time nice girls'. From the wizened old ladies outside the girlie bars; opticians in white coats; tall, thin Pakinstani men in elegant suits, there is a constant entreaty to trade.

In a moment of fateful hesitation I found myself staring at a leaflet which had just been thrust in my hand. It was for a reflexology foot massage. I was on the tail end of a gruelling few weeks of travel and it had crossed my mind that I should try something like this. Spotting the pause and the internal debate, a short round middle-aged Chinese lady wearing an old Chinese style smock and trousers and incongruously wearing Nike trainers, grabbed me by the arm.

'This way, this way it will be good,' she said pushing me towards a darkened doorway. 'You like! You see.' Perhaps it was the jet lag, perhaps it was the chance to see what lay behind the burning bright shops, but zombie-like I followed.

Inside there was a lobby lit by a single unadorned light swinging from the ceiling. A small plastic sign on the wall with an arrow pointing upwards read 'Kwang Tai Foot Reflexology Clinic Ltd'. At the end of a lobby there was a lift and I was more or less pushed into it. My captor pressed a button and the door crashed shut and rattling and banging, the lift started its journey upwards.

I had a momentary passing sense of doom. As we rose rather tentatively upwards I thought ruefully that I was about to enter the rather sinister and unknown territory I had been observing from the outside a few minutes earlier. What would I find beyond the clanking, shuddering lift doors? A seedy brothel or a ruthless bunch of thugs from the local Triad gang, capable of kidnapping and mindless, gratuitous violence?

But when the doors creaked open I found myself facing neither of these alternatives but instead a rather tatty looking white parrot. It glared and started walking purposefully towards me, rolling like an old gunfighter. My companion swung a badly aimed kick at it and it retreated inside a door and I was pushed in after it. Before I could collect my wits, she disappeared back inside the lift which groaned back into life.

I found myself inside a small disorderly room with a row of rather battered easy chairs along one wall with little stools in front of them. On the opposite wall was an enormous television. A lady of uncertain age came up and introduced herself as Winnie and showed me into one of the chairs. She then, presumably in deference to my origins, switched channels on the television to Pearl which was showing an American programme about the economics of Old Europe.

My anxiety subsiding, I looked around and wondered what I was supposed to do. There seemed to be two other customers in the place; both very overweight Chinese men. One seemed to be having something rather drastic done to his feet by a young girl who had a tray of what appeared to be scalpels, files and other instruments of torture next to her. The other was simply fast asleep, snoring deeply as the problems with Romanian tractor manufacturing were aired.

Winnie returned with a washing up bowl filled with what seemed like fairly strong tea. Sitting on the stool in front of me she took off my shoes and socks and put my feet into the liquid. It was warm rather than hot, not unpleasant.

'OK?' Winnie asked.

'More sugar?' I asked

'I come back when they ready!' She smiled, standing up.

Feeling somewhat incongruous, with my trouser legs rolled up and my feet in a plastic orange pan I looked around a little more. Jars lined the opposite wall next to the television with what I took to be aromatherapy oils. There were large numbers of blue files piled up around the floor. On another wall was a large poster of an enormous pair of feet – divided up in the way you see butchers' diagrams and labelled with Chinese characters. At the far end of the room two doorways led off to little massage rooms each containing a narrow table covered with an embroidered cloth. The ambience was neither of the bordello nor the clinic, but something much more domestic.

People kept arriving, and the hubbub rose in the room as all the chairs were filled. Winnie came back, retook her position on the little stool, lifted one foot out of the liquid, dried it and looked at it with professional interest. She then took one calloused knuckle and pushed it firmly into the sole of my foot. Not convinced she did it again and pushed even harder. Over the next twenty five minutes she pushed, pulled, poked and pressed my two feet, the sensations veering without warning between very pleasant to painful. At one moment she stopped and picking up each foot one after the other, swapping them back and forward and looking at me quizzically, enquired: 'You bad shoulder?'

Which I have.

'I fix.'

She finished with my feet, dried them and walked behind me and started on my head and shoulders. Somewhere over the last little while, accumulated stockpiles of frustration and confusion seemed to have ebbed away. In many ways I had the same sense of stillness as I had on my trek in Morocco. How could this be? Was it just podiatric bliss?

I looked around the now crowded narrow room. It was full of men and women sitting with their feet in buckets of warm tea, laughing, smiling chattering, in one or two cases holding hands. With the exception of the truculent parrot staring balefully in from the door everyone seemed infused with a sense of conviviality. Moreover I noted, they had come not on their own like me, but in twos and threes. Reflexology was clearly a social event. Perhaps a night out at the Kwong Tai Foot Reflexology Clinic was like the bar of an English pub, a place of intimacy and intercourse.

One thing I have noticed as a visitor to Hong Kong and Far East over many years is how convivial many normally formal and reserved Chinese men and women are when they are with close family or friends. From the way most of the clients were engaging at the Kwang Tai Foot Reflexology Clinic Ltd, they knew each other well.

Other, more rigorous, observers have noted this intense sociability. Chinese in Hong Kong, it is often claimed, are defined by a sense of mutuality which exists amongst family and a close group of others. People see themselves as defined by the web of relationships in which they exist. The idea of a completely separate self, one who might be nostalgically seeking a next-to world that they could more completely inhabit, might be a bizarre concept.

I bid adieu to Winnie and the parrot, paid and left the intimacy of the little clinic and went back out into the tumult of Tsim Sha Tsui. Alone and unafraid and fuelled by jetlag I walked for what seemed an age amongst the dark and the gaudy.

The sense of reverie established through the ministrations of Winnie remained as I wandered the streets as if in a transparent bubble, within and without the constant press of humanity. I delighted again in the exotic, sensuous assault of downtown Kowloon, the almost total overload of being there, until I was suddenly aware I was lonely. Lonely, in that bitter sweet way in which you can touch contentment or bliss or simply joy but can't taste it without a friend to share it with. In a weird way, that I do not fully understand, it was if I needed someone else within this experience, for me to be totally part of it myself. Even Florence the Moroccan mule would have sufficed.

I thought about the juxtaposition between the overcrowded awful conditions in which many people in Hong Kong live and the conviviality of the Kwang Tai Foot Reflexology Clinic. It is tempting always to think that we stay and accept things because we think we have no choice, because we are afraid but may be such limitations and adversity have their own accidental rewards that bind us also more firmly. Hardship and adversity often create a common endeavour and a struggle that must be shared. And this breeds companionship; an intense closeness that taps into our ancestral spirit of tribal membership.

For, as I watched the ebb and flow of peoples in these backstreets of humanity, this potential for companionship seemed endless. Palaeolithic nomads, hunter gatherers following the great migrations of beasts across the earth, or Neolithic settlers huddled against the cold waiting for the first crack of spring and the early shoots of the bearded barley. Whomever those in the crowd of a hot Tsim Sha Tsui night would call granddad or grandmother, had a common need to connect to others to survive and in doing so must also have been willing to surrender a little of themselves; to fit in, to be voluntary slaves to the social agreement that makes survival possible.

Companionship, I speculated reflects our tribal origins. We are of tribes, which shape who we are and the meaning we put on our universe. From tribes we evolved to communities which fulfilled a similar function. This must therefore be essential to who we are.

Companionship is the payback for fitting in. Companionship! How little regarded a quality of our existence it has become; poor second cousin to our ambition, our spiritual loftiness, our intelligence and our search for one true love. Its purpose is dismissed as the lesser one of ameliorating loneliness, the soft-eyed Labrador that sits by our feet in the solitude of our autumn days.

We applaud the separateness of ourselves, we are private heroes on an individual quest. But should that mean that emotional connection and openness of spirit can only lie behind the marriage door or in the whispered secrets of lovers? Maybe the desire to see ourselves as separate and unfolding is peculiarly strong in the west, making us undervalue the idea of companionship – the people we would share our bread with. The Chinese character for companionship also means artistry, skill, ability and wisdom. Is it fanciful to hear in this the echoes of the whole being greater than the sum of the parts? And the emotional strength that people can derive from it?

But defining ourselves by our separateness may also be spoken of in the east. There is an idea running through a strand of spiritual thinking that you must separate yourself from the emotional, messy world of relating to others, that a sense of fulfilment can be achieved only by a disconnection from them, a renunciation of the world.

Yet stubborn pagan remnants of companionship, our ancestral tribal nature, remain: the mothers at the early-morning school gate echoing the women washing clothes in a stream in Morocco, both engaged in a lively and sometimes uninhibited exchange. The content of these conversations is never just the latest fashion news or the exploits of a child but also occasional cries from the soul, the more intimate whispering of secrets telling of inadequate partners, joys, sadnesses, hopes and disappointments.

And this interaction is not just the stereotypical preserve of mothers and women. Men – soldiers, outlaws, miners, labourers, seamen, dockers, all have traditionally created a band of brothers usually united in adversity and adventure. No doubt, I thought, conversations amongst men, particularly in my Britain usually consist of inhibited joshing, but within them I have seen gruff acts of compassion, tongue-tied moments of inspiration and inarticulate words of wisdom.

Companionship requires trust to know people well enough so that you can open yourself to who you are. I have been liberated, rescued, enriched, inspired by those who for a while travelled with me as companions and I have echoed in an empty well where our roads have parted. It has been the arm around my shoulder from the most inhibited of friends when I learned of my mother's catastrophic illness, it has been the person I have laughed with until we wept, it has reminded me I was a better fighter when I was out for the count. My companions and their wonderful willingness to enter into creating a shared story have enabled me, even when in the end I have to complete that particular story on my own.

Friendship is a hardy flower that flourishes in adversity, close proximity and tough times. This must be part of the way people survive or even thrive in places such as the high rise sweating apartments of places like Mong Kok.

Is companionship a fading light behind the suburban hygiene of closed doors, closed curtains and little hedges which separate out our lives? If so we mourn it because this separates us from part of who we are. In an age where we leave our village, our family and friends, not once but several times in the course of our lives, we can become disjointed from this source of strength. Are rising divorce rates the inevitable consequence of our increasing remoteness from each other? And does all this make us afraid of taking the steps that we want to take? So does a lack of companionship paradoxically inhibit the development of who we might be? If we move in a world where we trust too few, can we develop the necessary companionship for life's journey – a circle of sisters or a band of brothers?

As I reflected on it, I concluded that our modern dilemma is that we lose both our freedom *and* our source of companionship. We live in a kind of limbo unclear of who we are, neither defined by an internal sense of who we are becoming nor through connection with those around us. Psychologists have shown our judgement of who our best friends are is based upon those who support most fully our sense of identity.

Knulp senses this. He never stays far from the places where people live, edging out of lives which are often troubled and difficult – drawn like a moth around a flame to the light source of companionship. Despite his freedom, he continually circles back, he cannot totally leave the tribe.

Ending up back on the waterfront I gazed out at the magnificent skyline of Hong Kong at night. Without companions I thought, we would have no stories nor people to tell them to.

CHAPTER NINE

The Old Bank

The third kind of slave was the ancestor of today's ambitious executive and bureaucrat
Theodore Zeldin, An Intimate History of Humanity

Sitting in the middle of the 'face' – position, respect, propriety – of Hong Kong, is the great totem-uncle of the Wayfoong, known to westerners as the Hong Kong Shanghai Banking Corporation. The Bank.

Nowadays banks come across as almost unhinged in their avarice and lack of responsibility. It seems an age ago that banks were the epitome of prescribed action, disciplined thought and conservative expectations – the potentates of commerce where life was measured out by regulation and procedure, column and signature. Perhaps these days, most banks are just pirate gangs without the sex appeal, but there was a time when that old fashioned value of your word being your bond meant something.

If anything captured this world of caution and probity it could be argued that it was HSBC – the Home of Scottish Banking Clerks – here in Hong Kong. Founded to finance trade with China it was famously conservative, reserved and at least on first acquaintance, rather formal. It was said that in the past, in the very strict pecking order of position in Hong Kong, the Chairman of the bank was slightly above that of the Governor General of the colony. I was assured, with the utmost sincerity by one old china hand, that the traffic lights were so arranged that they were never on red as his chauffeured car swept him into headquarters at One Queens Road Central.

Staring out across the water at its famous red hexagon sign, I thought to myself this was *voluntary* slavery incarnate. Traditionally, you had to ask the manager's permission to get married, and it was rumoured, to remove your jacket required board level approval. The niceties of social position were strictly observed. Extreme poverty, might take the voluntary out of the slavery, in the mine, on the production line, in the sweat shop, but surely becoming a bank manager was a decision made amongst options, any of which would bring rewards and security?

And yet, for over a hundred years, people, mostly men, volunteered and journeyed from around the world to work there. Why? And why did they stay on for years with contracts that bound them for more than a third of a lifetime?

Here in HSBC's natural territory of cultural collision, financial ambition and intelligence, I wondered at the potential attractions of surrender. On the surface, it might be quite simple: voluntary slavery in banks can make you rich and offer you the good things in life.

Surrendering, at least in part one's independence and freedom of action, has always been a route to material advancement, perversely higher status, power and first class seats. The eunuch and chief slave could command at least the behavioural respect of those whose craved benediction and access.

So, ironically, slavery can give access to status and power. As Theodore Zeldin notes: '*The Ottoman and Chinese empires were often managed by slaves, sometimes by eunuch slaves, who rose to the highest posts and indeed sometimes ended as grand viziers and emperors*'.

But I suspected there was more to it than this. I had sensed amongst the boys from the old days whom I had met over the years – the HSBC old guard – that something more subtle than that was going on, a more multi-dimensional reality beyond the trading of freedom for money.

Old boys such as Ollie, collector of military hardware, fine carpets, ancient Chinese motor cars, and a long-time loyal, diffident and diligent servant of HSBC.

We had met after he found me admiring the Chinese carved windows in the HSBC mess on Mong Kok on one my previous trips to the region. The windows are large frames made up of exquisite intricate carvings of rural images in a kind of lace effect so that when backed by paper the light could be let through (the inventive Chinese never made glass). It turned out Ollie had collected them himself from the mainland and hung them against the grey walls to add a touch of decoration and sophistication.

My enthusiasm had led to a memorable meeting with his Chinese wife, drinking rather fine wine, and appreciating several more of the wooden windows he had collected on a recent trip to the mainland. The evening had concluded with me buying one of them, a large panel of carved hay sheaves, bats and songbirds, leaving it to the sobriety of the following morning to try to work out how to get it back to England on an aeroplane.

He was what used to be known as International Officer. He had worked for nearly thirty years on a contract of employment, in which he could be and was, moved at twenty-four hours' notice, almost like Army Officer. Such moves could see him one day in steamy Brunei and the next in the eye-burning dry heat of Riyadh in the centre of Saudi Arabia.

If anyone knew about the pleasures of voluntary slavery it would be Ollie, so I arranged to meet up with him a couple of evenings later. We met at a favourite haunt of his: the Foreign Correspondents' Club of Hong Kong. As I watched him winding his way back from the bar with a couple of beers, I noted to myself the fact he was also winding his way to the end of a long and peripatetic career with the old bank, a career that had included time in China during its more repressive moments, Saudi Arabia, the Middle East as well as Asia.

'So Ollie,' I said after we had clinked our glasses and taken a first sip. 'Tell me about the old days, what was it like working here?'

'The Bank?'

'Yeah, this has been your life.'

Ollie thought about it for a while, ummed and aahed, considering the question, formed several angles, held one answer in his hand but discarded it, found another, then launched in.

'You had to be aware of your place, do what was expected of you. But under the surface it was much more...' he searched for a word, '... even. You see, despite all the hierarchy and protocol – you weren't allowed to get married for the first five years you worked here – you were expected to make things happen, not just push a piece of paper around.

'You took responsibility for sorting things out – particularly if customers were involved. No good sitting back and waiting for someone else to fix it. There was a belief there would and should be a solution, you were expected to find it, whatever the problem.'

'Whatever the problem?' I asked. He thought for a second searching for an example.

'Take this branch in Brunei, years ago it was, the manager went to open the safe in the morning. One of those old jobs – needed a key. Put the key in and found it wouldn't go in properly. Wiggles it around – no way! – couldn't open the safe. Peers in the lock; couldn't see a thing; gets a match – a damn great bug has crawled in and died. Nasty thing stopping the lock from working. The Bank had to open but the safe wouldn't.

'Now the word got around that the Bank had no money. Panic grew and people started coming in demanding their cash. People were getting really agitated, shouting and trying to push to the front. The bank staff were attempting to calm people down and explain that their money was safe but the safe door was stuck. All options were being tried to sort the problem out, but nothing was working. What do you do ...? A hundred people banging on the door asking for their cash!

'Someone tried to entice the bug out with a noodle but of course it was dead! It was getting all rather hairy when this young lad came up to the counter and said he thought he could help. He was taken to talk to the manager. The boy explained that his brother knew someone who was currently serving a prison sentence as a safe cracker.

'Being an HSBC officer, and well connected, the manager was on good terms with the Head of Police – phones him up and asks if he could borrow the villain for a short while. No problem said the police chief. Happy to oblige. A short time later, a police van, armed escort and safe cracker arrived at the Bank. It took the safe cracker less than half an hour to open the safe. Back to the clink for him and the bank could get on with business as usual.

'Probably not the first manager to break into his own safe, but done with the best of intentions.' He laughed.

I chuckled, but what about the rules, I wondered. HSBC had appeared tied up in rules and regulations surely they made life tedious and frustrating? Ollie thought for a moment.

'Yes in many respects it was,' he said. 'Everyone expected that things should be done properly and to policy. There was a massive amount of trust that you would follow these rules. I got in trouble for buying the wrong sort of car once. But even then...' Ollie smiled at the memory, '... people could play the rules like a favourite violin.

'There was one character. He worked in Head Office but also had to cover in Thailand for his deputy who was off sick. One of deputy's customers felt he had been treated badly and he inherited this continuing argument. With all correspondence on sensitive matters, a copy would be made as a managerial letter and it would be logged in Head Office by the senior officer. So the guy sent a rude managerial letter from Head Office to the No 2's office, knowing he would be there as a locum to pick it up. When he arrived, he received the letter and sent a thoroughly rude letter back to himself in Head Office. He continued to escalate the argument, until the Chairman, told him to stop it!'

Ollie, stood up. 'Another drink?' and before I had time to demur, wandered off, stopping en route to talk to someone.

I sipped my drink, stretched my legs and looked around. The place was buzzing with accents and languages. Although there is nothing that remarkable about the décor and the style – the *fact* of the Foreign Correspondents' Club loomed large. It was founded as a refuge for correspondents expelled from China after the Communist Party seized power and closed their club in Shanghai. During the Vietnam War, correspondents covering the grim conflict would retreat here for some rest and recuperation. It has been described as a 'noisy bastion of free speech, gossip and hard drinking'. Perhaps somewhere in the bar tonight, possibly over one hundred years old, might be Claire Hollingworth, the legendary British foreign correspondent for *The Daily Telegraph*. She covered World War II and Vietnam and much else that was dangerous and violent, and famously broke the story of the German invasion of Poland simply by coming home late from a party one night and seeing German tanks ready to move.

I remembered having lunch with a guy once who had been airlifted off his own bank to escape a rioting mob. Just the sort of story the members would cover. And a conversation with another which I had dismissed at the time as a bit of a yarn. He had started his managerial career running a small branch in one of the smaller Gulf States. Actually his branch, he told me, was a caravan, he lived in the back of it and used the front to deal with the public. At the time, a civil war involving rifle-bearing horsemen was going on around him. The occasional shot whistled through the window whilst he hid under the table.

The Old Bank from this point of view seemed closer in spirit, I mused, to this place of hacks, newshounds and story grubbers, than the church-like hallowed halls of corporate finance. In the dust of the ledgers it seemed, was the DNA of derry-doing, a potential for serious escapades albeit dressed in the pinstripe of deference and the pince-nez of elitism. As if on cue, Ollie returned.

'Sorry about that Steve, I hadn't seen that chap for years. We bumped into each other way back during the revolution in 1967. Things in Hong Kong were very tense then.' Ollie explained that all the house staff were security people back then and that some had been arrested. They had been exciting times, with shoot-outs between rival groups supporting the Chinese and the British. There were slogans exclaiming the British were wicked and crushing the people, and that Hong Kong Bank was bad. As Ollie had been in the TA, he had to join the military and spent six months as a radio operator, which was where he had met the guy at the bar. It was lucky it hadn't got out of hand, he mused.

'There were curfews and even a few bombs. Strangest thing at the time was that the CIA were supporting Taiwanese militants that our British CID were trying prevent stirring up trouble. It had been difficult to know who was after whom.'

I was rapidly changing my perceptions of what banking used to be like – whatever happened to boring, sober and tedious! Ollie looked a bit crestfallen, as if he had committed the cardinal British sin of not making everything seem mundane and low key.

'Sorry old boy, some of the time it was very ordinary. You knew what was expected and did your duty. But things were not always straightforward. You had to be able to manage the downright difficult and unexpected.

'Take the Shanghai posting back when things were really bad and edgy. You were a kind of hostage, you weren't allowed to leave China until someone else arrived to replace you.'

He described the run-down office in Shanghai, infested with cockroaches which still managed to keep going despite the government efforts to make life difficult. Ollie was one of the managers and the average age of the staff was over seventy-five. They had survived the turmoil and knew to attend the weekly party meetings and not appear too friendly with foreigners. One day there had been a knock at the door and a member of staff came in. 'There's someone to see you,' he had said. 'But you won't want to see him so I'll wait here, count to ten, and then say sorry we can't help.'

This had aroused Ollie's interest and he decided he was going to see this 'someone'. 'Bring him in,' he'd said. Moments later, in walked a European in Chinese clothes. His name was Sergei, a white Russian. He explained he had been a journalist and had been arrested during the purge. He had been in prison for thirty years, charged with being a spy, and had been released that morning. He was in a desperate state with no finger nails, but still alive and all he had were the clothes he stood up in. He had an account with the bank, but with pre-liberation money, which was worthless if you were deemed a suspicious character, and he could not establish a bone fide to exchange the money for yen.

'You couldn't sling him out,' said Ollie. 'So we had a whip round to give him some cash that day. We looked after him and found him a job at the Foreign Institute teaching Russian. We also found out that he had a daughter living in Australia. We spoke to people in the Australian Embassy and after some negotiation, they agreed to find him a space in an old folks home in Sydney where he ended up helping the Ozzie's with his insights into the Chinese way of thinking.'

Afterwards, on my way back to my hotel via the Star Ferry, watching the incredible skyline of Hong Kong soar in to the night sky and the watery bustle of Fragrant Harbour, I couldn't help thinking the experiences of my own life, which although driven by a supposed maverick tendency, seemed rather timid and shallow in comparison to Ollie's universe. I remembered a conversation with my good friend Linet one night in Oxford months before. We had been talking about the extent to which one should conform and do what is expected when your inclination was to do otherwise. My probably contemptuous argument was that we fitted in because in the end people were afraid of their dangerous edge, putting safety and security above identity in terms of who they wanted to be. Linet had disagreed,

'It's not like that for me, it's more that I find rules liberating in the sense that they create a level playing field which means everyone (including me) has the same opportunities.'

'But following rules, doing what is expected may mean we end up denying who we actually are!'

'There has always been a bit of an anarchist streak in you,' she said kindly, putting a reassuring hand on my arm. 'I know that anarchists suggest that people are then freer to be kind, take responsibility for their own actions do what's right etc but in the end anarchy means that the strongest wins …'

I'd protested at the time this wasn't about strength, it was about identity but now I thought about the point she made from a different perspective. Perhaps voluntary slavery in a strange way provided a kind of protective frame. It puts the tiger back in the cage and enables us to do things that we would usually be inhibited about.

Thinking about the conversation with Ollie, for at least some of the managers the rewards of working for an organisation seemed rich and varied. The world Ollie described was vital, adventurous, fun even.

And companionable.

I had already discovered the interconnectedness of the managers in the old bank. People were god parents to each other's children, friends for life, best men at each other's weddings.

And self sacrificing…

Sir Vandeleur (Tubby) Grayburn was the General Manager of the then Hong Kong Shanghai Banking Corporation when Hong Kong fell to the Japanese attack during the Second World War. Refusing the escape route offered, he preferred instead to stay with his staff to try and protect them as much as possible. Arrested for breaking the strict Japanese regulations – he was funding and organising supplies to be smuggled into the internment camps – he was imprisoned in brutal conditions and died of starvation and neglect in the prison hospital.

The old bank was no doubt hard-nosed, tough and elitist and represents a distant place and a distant time but the possibility it seemed to offer, of being an *adventurous slave*, was an intriguing one.

As I was swept ashore by the human tide exiting the Star Ferry, I reasoned that beyond the façade of assumptions and stereotypes, a more complex richer proposition had existed and could still. It is not enough to divide the world simply into slaves and buccaneers as if they were complete alternatives; 'fitting in' respects and responds to deep human needs. Fleetingly I wondered whether perhaps our nostalgia for freedom is mere wilfulness after all. Fitting in seems to offer not just safety but the possibility of adventure and much more. Is the derry-doing banker a mirror image of the scholarly buccaneer?

And therefore are freedoms to be inconsistent, to be present and evolve – the begetters of nostalgia – simply the remnant notions of immature strivings?

But then as I disembarked at Kowloon and walked across out from the terminal, I noticed a handbill, balletic in the evening breeze. Stooping to pick it up I saw it had been left by the people who stand every day, generally ignored by the pressing throng, protesting against the treatment by the Chinese mainland authorities of members of a movement called the Falun Gong, a sect founded in the last years of the twentieth century in communist China. With a set of ideas and propositions strange to westerners, it had grown to be embraced by millions. The reaction of the Chinese government to this non-fitting-in had been thorough and vicious. Freedom does matter I thought. It is not enough to simply accept someone else's rule book, someone else's obligations. It matters that we have a sense of ourselves unbound from the convention and order and place of the world around us. Evolving away from what is expected is elemental to our individuality and through that, the societies we live in. If there is a difference between an adventurous and an audacious life it is the latter that involves some breaking of the rules or defying of expectation.

'Knulp,' I wondered aloud. 'You were an adventurer, weren't you. Were you audacious?'

'Difficult to say,' I thought I heard him reply. 'Many people thought I should be someone else. Is not doing so a breaking of the rules?'

CHAPTER TEN

Turn Sideways Into the Sun

I am a part of all that I have met;
Yet all experience is an arch wherethro'
Gleams that untravell'd world,

Alfred Lord Tennyson, Ulysses

Relegated from the womb-like experience of first class for the return journey, I sat back with the press of humanity. I watched listlessly as the aircrew endeavoured to persuade us to watch the instructions on what we had to do if our 747 had to make an improbable landing, graceful as a swan, on the chilly waters of the Arctic Ocean.

The plane had filled with the usual cross section of humanity that makes up business and tourist travel. Sons and daughters of Scottish crofters, nomadic merchants along the Silk Road, Dutch pastors, Russian Jews, Spanish aristocrats, Hugenot rebels, Samurai warriors, Chinese Christians, Lancashire millworkers, all products at least in part of the communities in which they were ancestrally born. But also in their suits and holiday clothes refugees or fugitives from that, or nothing would have changed.

Everyone on this plane I imagined, had been brought up to ignore things and deny things. The rich possibility of the world and the shimmering mirrors of next-to worlds give us brief compelling glimpses of who else we might be prompting in our natural restlessness. At that moment we are ready to change ourselves or even change the world. But a society and a community shrinks from such abandon and trains us to resist such fancies, lest we become inconsistent, unpredictable and disruptive. The process is more subtle. It is often less the brutal oppression of the state, society or community that the anarchists, drop-outs and outsiders rail against – rather than that our nature and upbringing has built in to us its own defence in the form of experiencing the deep rewards of fitting in.

Sitting in the back of the plane it became as clear as it could be that an essential paradox of our existence is that we are both part of the story of the communities into which we are born and potentially renegades and exiles from it. We are forever seeking ways to resolve the tension between the two opposite ways of being. Between being captured into the story into which we are born and writing a new and potentially dangerous story for ourselves. Between the freedoms of the moment, of inconsistency of authentic evolution and the pleasures of companionship, belongingness and the safety of the tribe. To choose one way only is to wish away an essential part of ourselves.

An *essential* dilemma, core to our being and our identity.

And looking at the polyglot diversity of my fellow passengers I ruminated that this must be both a personal phenomenon and shared experience. And an ongoing one through the course of history, or we wouldn't have one. And different societies probably generate different ways of trying to order its members in the light of this dilemma.

As the stewardesses, like well-to-do and well-appointed nurses, turned out lights, fetched water and closed shutters, or proffered a last whisky, I recalled reading Richard Nisbett's view in a book called *The Geography of Thought*, that the individualism of the west and the idea of the individual as a separate agent arose from the position of early Greece as a busy, coastal trading nation in which they were '*constantly encountering novel and perplexing peoples, religions and polities … Athens itself would have been rather like the bar in Star Wars*'. Greeks were constantly confronted by contradiction, a diversity of views emphasising the separateness of people and objects.

In old China on the other hand, the need to farm rice in an environment on relatively flat fertile plains where planned irrigation was an important feature, encouraged collaboration and co-ordination. Add to this a people who were very largely of the same ethnic tribe and a geography, low mountains and navigable rivers that enabled centralised control, then you end up with a very different way of dealing with the world. In China, people are defined in terms of their relationship with each other and the impetus for everyone is to establish and maintain harmony. People do not regard themselves so strongly as separate entities – there is no real Chinese word for 'self'. The dilemma still remains but culturally it will be dealt with in quite different ways.

Sometime after my return from Hong Kong, I had the opportunity to explore further the idea of how our cultures wrap themselves around us and our nostalgia-inducing dilemmas. Cilian Fennel is a former producer on Irish television. Speechwriter, communications guru and deeply passionate about all things Celtic and beyond the pale, we had met at a conference on storytelling in Copenhagen and got on well, sharing a mutual skittishness about some of the more 'right on' aspects of the conference menu and agreed to meet up later.

Later proved to be a trip to Dublin. The deal was we would meet up at a place, which to me, was as close as it could be to an entrance hall to a next-to world: the Lincoln's Inn near St Stephen's Green. I had drunk there on several occasions more than twenty years ago. My memory in tableaux was of a long narrow bar serving a riotous mix of students, academics, would-be poets and the ghost of Nora Barnacle. It was of that uniquely Irish mix of high flown language and base desire that makes up a session. Sitting there talking blasphemy, bollocks, and Behan, as the black stuff and the pink lemonade flowed, I reckoned I was the closest I had ever been to being truly in my element: once, I was chatted up by a pretty girl who offered to take me back to her room to show me how to play the Peruvian nose flute.

A memory like this becomes a reference point for life; a place with which to contrast a more mundane current existence. Free of the bonds of ongoing experience, it is not locked in the past but is a timeless next-to world which you could, at any time, re-enter if you could only get around to it.

But not now. For when we go there, I found my next-to-world had been renovated! Everything was tasteful, clean, wannabe fashionable.

Hygienic.

The bar had been moved from running along the right hand side to being at the far end of the cellared room giving the place the feeling of the nave of a church. As Cilian and I made our way passed the vacant chairs and tables towards the bar/altar at which a bored barman/priest polished a beer glass, I could not help thinking that I had entered the halls of heaven and found them empty.

'The past is never what is was,' Cilian murmured sympathetically. 'It's one of its characteristics. You'd better have a whisky.'

Was it ever thus?

Later in more convivial surroundings, Cilian and I talked of nostalgia, this sense of possibility, the road not taken that had haunted me and it seems so many others.

'I used to think, it was me,' I confessed. 'But I'm beginning to think it's a bit bigger than that.'

And then, with the spirit of the old Lincoln Inn rising, I was suddenly into the key of late night conjecture in which I can excel: something half-formed which suddenly seems clearer – that our notions of magic, myth, legend and next-to worlds are not just cultural expressions of our nostalgic dilemmas, but are a kind of safety valve to deal with them.

In every age and place, people feel that there are other worlds running almost in parallel to the one we daily experience. This is not like heaven, a world to be experienced 'after' a life here, provided you have been good and dutiful, but a world that kind of motors alongside. And often these are worlds which are inhabited, not by us, but beings recognisably like us but different. In Morocco, it is the Djinn, in Europe the fairies, our folk memory captured and emasculated in the form of children's tales: Narnia, Wonderland, Avalon across the Western Sea.

The line in between the two has always been blurred. For instance the Djinns, from Morocco to Zanzibar, have existed as everyday reality, albeit parallel reality to human kind from time immemorial. These spirits of fire, the various names of which give us: demon, ghoul as well as genie, were woven into the teachings of Mohammed. The Djinns are not ghosts, they exist in everyday North African society.

'It seems next-to worlds are a universal phenomenon,' I mused. I think we rather dismiss them at our peril. The fact that people still believe in them, are drawn to them, reflects something about who we are and how we deal with the world. I guess it's a kind of pseudo rationality to dismiss them as if they could not, must not shape our experience. What do you think Cilian, am I talking rubbish or what?'

'No, you're not. At least not this time. Ireland is a great place for stories of next-to-worlds,' Cilian said. 'We've got several, we're full of tales that tell of humans wandering into the Otherworld, and of the supernatural visiting us. You can't help but bump in to them,' he said. 'For instance there is a field near Croghan, site of Maeve's kingdom, and there is a bush, an unremarkable bush at that, which covers the entrance to an underground cave of about 120ft long. This is a portal to the Otherworld which used to open at Samhai, Hallowe'en to you, and allow the spirits to come out and mingle for the day.'

'That's it,' I said. 'There's always a door, a rabbit hole, a wardrobe...'

He told me of Tír na nÓg, the land of eternal youth, not of this world but at the edges of it. Plenty, all in one place: strength, laughter, drink, love, poetry: the idyllic macrocosm of which the Lincoln's Inn had once been the micro.

Here fled the ancient Tuatha De Danaan. 'Our most artistic ancestors,' said Cilian.

There are several accounts of how they came to be there. According to Cilian they had been tricked by the Gael, the first men in Ireland. But my favourite explanation, I heard told by the poet David Whyte. Once of this world, they had found themselves facing yet another battle against the crude, encroaching armies of men. On the day of the final battle they massed on the crest of a hill and as dawn broke turned sideways into the sun and disappeared.

In our mythology and folk tales these next-to-worlds tempt because they hold what is beautiful, that which we want but feel we cannot have. To these we are inevitably in some way drawn. Their inhabitants are unrestrained, very tiny, very large, very wicked or truly good in some way. They are places of abundance. They contain our hopes and our nightmares.

But you visit them at your peril for the stories often tell of what happens to you on return: you turn to stone, come back to find your lover an aged old crone. Oisin rides back from Tír na nÓg with his lover and guide Niamh and before she can stop him alights from his horse and ages to dust in an instant.

So we also seem to be hard-wired to fear going there, despite its temptations. The message we hear and tell ourselves seems to be 'don't part belong, best stay at home, avoid the arcane and the conjuring of the wizard, the wild horses and the little people. If you go, you can't come back. Be steady, be cautious, dream but don't act, wait till next year, wait till when …'

And so we stay. Put down roots. Get a mortgage. Banish our restlessness to the edge of the night.

But then Knulp comes tapping at our door, we sit him by the

fire, ask for a story, a song, let him begin to play and as our feet tap a little, our head nods, and we remember how it was once and how it will ever be.

In a next-to world?

These stories tug at us because they reflect things we recognise, aspects of who we are: our sense of possibility, our procrastination, the injunction not to stray, the stranger who makes us feel restless. And I can't help thinking they offer something more than a dream of riches and some sort of power, for it is a nostalgia for *freedom*, whatever that may be, that Knulp evokes, not a lust for gold and other rewards. I began to understand that these legends and stories about next-to worlds are geographies of the mind. They are psychological as much as mythical. They are ways of exploring who we are and the steps that we take. Cilian told me these places captured the way we tend to bury our inner poet. Next-to worlds are a kind of call to us to evolve and regenerate, they are a real experience that is why they are so embedded in our culture. Art, I am coming to believe, is essentially about capturing new perspectives on the paradox of our existence. Artists are Knulp-like characters, creating a bridge from the tribal way we see the world to another reflection of the possibilities within it.

From the images created thirty-five thousand years ago in a Shamanic pulse and trance on the walls of Chauvet in France, to the stuff hanging from the ceiling of the Tate Modern, all capture the fleeting glimpses of possibility from a next-to world. Cilian would probably say Ireland itself, the possibility of it, was conjured by writers, playwrights and painters, from the myths and legends and folk memories of a another past.

The momentum behind this insight continued when I met up finally with the one of the people who had prompted my nostalgic search – Jason Webster. He lives in Valencia, in Spain, a place where, I suspected, all the paradox and colour of my adventure might shine most brightly.

I had not met Jason before, the photograph on the dust cover of his book had shown a youngish, blond-haired guy in a black T-shirt, blue jeans, arms folded, wearing Police sunglasses – not exactly the Englishman of letters, whatever such a man should look like.

We met at the Artereo Mercantile, in the Plaza del Ayuntamiento. Whilst Jason, who did look more or less like his picture, fetched me a coffee in an attempt to wind back the traumas of the flight, I gazed through the windows of the cool, dark, rather austere inner space at the exuberant and imposing town hall across the street in the intense sunlight. It was bedecked in the yellow and red flags of the region. And seemed to dance in the heat. It contrasted with the building in which we sat which was sombre and rather austere – used it seems to discuss business and sober affairs. I sat in a place without colour or excessive ornament behind a grey glass window on the other side of which raged colour, activity, movement, vitality.

The idea of a world built of possibility and paradox and how that shapes our experience, appealed to Jason. He saw its reflection in Spain.

'This is a country which can be incredibly cruel, look at what happened during the civil war, but on the other hand,' he said looking outside into the plaza, 'if someone collapsed in the street everyone would rush to help. If you are travelling and things go wrong, sooner or later Samaritan-like, a stranger will stop and make all the problems go away.'

It was the intensity of Spain he loved, everything is done fully and valued. It is seen in the colours, the buildings, the light, the ceremony, the formality, the dance, the music. It's a place of passions.

'The thing is, Steve,' he said after a moment's silence, 'I am living in a country just in touch with another world, where fairy tales and reality and so on haven't become so separated. I feel I am living in a world that hasn't yet been completely taken over by the Enlightenment, if you see what I mean?'

'A sort of a superficial reality?' I suggested. 'The rather touching *faith* that in explaining human affairs you can ignore the magic going on in people's heads.'

'And ignore all the many things that were shaping a moment, it is still hard to do that in Spain.'

We ate at Le Pepica, one of the restaurants on the beach. Over a hundred years old it captures that unique intersection of formality and flamboyance that seems to characterise Spanish style. Big, almost cavernous, the interior was cool and subdued, opening out to a terrace and the fierce light of the beach. The blue and white tiled walls are covered with black and white photographs of the famous people who had eaten there, including of course Hemingway.

'I think Hemingway ate and drank everywhere didn't he?' I wondered aloud.

'Not necessarily,' said Jason. 'There is a bar along the coast called, in Spanish, "Hemingway didn't drink here"!'

I let Jason order, it's his town. Over the next six hours, we ate tapas and Paella, drank a beer or two, a bottle of wine and a brandy each. I particularly liked the Valencian dish: Esgarraet, a plate of roasted red peppers, salted cod and on this occasion dried tuna covered in rich, dense, Spanish olive oil.

Our conversation ranged loose and wild over many subjects as we were caught in its weft and warp, references and allusions to the same notions: that the culture of Spain was shaped in the interdependence of opposites, whisperings of paradox to be managed are present and close to the surface.

Take that most machismo of sports, bull fighting. Jason argued that yes it was a blood-letting ritual with its connotations of masculinity and domination, but it was also something else, something else equally ancient.

'It's the contest between man-sun-bull and woman-moon-toreador: with the woman coming out on top, are echoes of ancient matriarchal society. The closer the tearing sharp horns of the enraged bull are allowed to get to the manhood of the toreador, the louder the olé of the crowd.'

'But do people still see this?' I wondered. 'Or do they just see an angry bull and a skilful and foolishly brave matador?'

'Toreador,' corrected Jason.

Do they, does anyone really these days, connect beyond the given?

'Perhaps that's why Spain is still different,' he offered. 'One thing here is you get attention. This is not an atomised society, people connect. If you are on your own, go out shopping, go to the market. There will be someone, just selling potatoes, olives, perhaps a knife sharpener. Stop, talk, buy and you will get real attention. Not "have a nice day now" attention, real attention.'

The quality of attention – it is something to seek I said. We are so shorn of the ability to attend, what we see is what we expect to see and what we expect to see is something we learn from the worlds into which we are born. The Spain that Jason illuminated had not been painted over, the steam of history still crept up through the cracks. Chatting to him over the long hot hours of a Mediterranean afternoon, I had a growing sense that when I compared my experience of the evolving world in which I travelled and engaged with that of Spain, and what lay just below the surface, we might be rapidly losing touch with the multi-layered reality that surrounds us and substituting it with an ersatz, two dimensional 'I-World'. Here, cartoon-like next-to worlds are drawn without scent or nuance, tone or shade. Here gesture replaces depth and potency. It would be a bitter nostalgia if we emasculate our humanity by ignoring the world we are given and substituting a different sort of unreal one.

In flourishing as individuals and societies, more than any other beast, we have learned to respond to this potential of the world. Despite our blinkers, despite our prejudice we *do* see the possibilities of things. Our beliefs, our culture, our art even, arise from a visceral connection with the world.

Our mythologies, cultures and art capture and help shape our response to this universal challenge. When should we be a voluntary slave and when a buccaneer? And creatively this is not a one-off solution. We are not resolvable to a fixed point for we are engaged in an ongoing relationship, almost like a conversation, with a world that is itself full of potential and paradox.

To be a creative human being is to be nostalgic and restless.

CHAPTER ELEVEN

The Rules of The Road

Stormbound tied, up to the quay,
Moored up with a cargo of chances
Steve Bonham, *Somewhere in the Blue*

Knulp and I sat on the crest of a dune. The sun was beginning to slip into an infinite procession of sands and haze. On the ridge in front of us, Nick, in his strange green overalls and his Jordanian Bedouin scarf, sat in meditative contemplation of the evening journey from intense piercing almost white to the coming embraces of pink and indigo.

Down below us, small and still was the camp. We could make out the bodies sleeping in the late afternoon after the day's exertions, a trail of smoke rose from Saleh's cooking fire. Two of the Bedouin were kneeling behind one of the 4x4s, responding to the call to prayers. A little way from the others, I could see the figures of Marie, and Robert Twigger, in deep conversation. In the still air I could hear Marie's wholehearted laugh and could imagine her wide grin and Robert's slightly perplexed answering smile.

On the crest of seeming nothingness, I let time slip by. This would be the last time I would be in the desert for some time and I did not know when I would return. I reasoned that the more still I was, the slower time would pass.

'So where have I got,' I wondered. 'Where has nostalgia taken me?'

'Egypt?' suggested Knulp.

From the continuing momentum of happenstance this was the eighth trip I had made this year and the desert had become the deep well from which I could refresh my soul. It had been love at first sight – a man finding his environment. The catalyst had been the request by a large organisation to build 'a new way of looking and acting in the world amongst our leaders' as part of a leadership development program which integrated the cognitive, clever, analytic world of commercial endeavour, with the need to understand yourself more fully and others within it if you were to be a truly effective leader.

The magician who could make this happen turned out to be Robert Twigger, an adventurer and exponent of the art of do-it-yourself exploration. We had met when I had visited Cairo where he now lives with his wife and two children. He can be the most original of company and his blog and books ruminate on just about everything from the importance of owning a shed, how to eat Puffer fish and thoughts on a universal language. Moreover he has paddled across Canada in a birch bark canoe, caught the world's longest snake and been entertained by real Zombies in Haiti.

It was Robert who first took me into the desert. Back in February. He had come by the hotel in El Maadi where I was staying, the night after we had met and had dinner. He was looking slightly worried, emphasising – with his grey-hair and beard and round-lensed glasses – an air of being more a university lecturer than an explorer.

'We got a problem, a bit of one with my car. I just got back from the desert yesterday. It was idling very fast. I can't fix it. I've tried to get another one but the driver hasn't turned up. We could risk it, we might break down but I've got my satellite phone, it would be a bit of a wait perhaps, no more than a couple of days…'

Feeling slightly concerned, I climbed into the passenger seat of his beaten up short wheel based Toyota land cruiser. Twigger is inordinately proud of this vehicle. He devotes nearly an entire chapter to it in one of his more recent books. As we snaked out through the insane traffic of Cairo, demonstrating the driving style that one might call *native*, he cheerfully told me that this version of the vehicle would be more or less illegal anywhere else but here.

The preparation for this programme involved several other more long lasting trips into the Sahara, but I will never forget the emotional impact of the first moment we pulled off the road drove a little way to the edge of an escarpment, got out of the 4x4 and stood in convivial silence staring into an infinity of heat, barrenness and momentousness.

So began a relationship with the desert and the friendship with Robert that continues in its idiosyncratic way.

The exploratory trips had been carried out first of all by Robert and me, and then with Marie my companion from Morocco and finally making a party of four, the ex-actor, personal development guru and delver into things spiritual Nick 'the Desert'.

With the help of members of a Bedouin tribe who have worked with Robert on some seriously tough trips into parts of the Sahara virtually undiscovered, we put together a trip in which we could take the leaders out into the desert for a couple of days with sufficient levels of ambiguity, strain and challenge and in a region far enough away from the beaten track, to make sure than there was little chance it would be considered a tourist excursion.

For the work itself, our clients were transported in 4x4s adapted for the desert, but for the four of us, we had to make do with more basic arrangements. In April the trips were made in Twigger's battered old Toyota land cruiser; the October trips in Hamdi's more spacious (and more recent) long wheel based version.

Each trip was more or less identical. We assembled in the hotel car park at 5:55am, with a bleary-eyed group displaying a mix of enthusiasm and truculence. Hamdi and Saleh organised the transfer and securing of tents, camp polls, sleeping bags, boxes of water, cooking gear and several cool boxes containing lunch, ice, beer and wine, cans of drink, logs and food, as far as possible splitting the load onto the roof racks or two or three 4x4s. They were aided by two or three other Bedouin.

Also standing around, would be a silent Dr Nabil or his colleague Dr Ayman – happily bemused to receive a handsome payment for sitting all day in a Bedouin camp looking after a flask of anti-snake bite serum and to be the recipient of no more than the occasional enquiry concerning a sore throat.

Always, always the departure would be delayed by the arrival of the tourist police and the subsequent farrago of handshakes, smiles, pointing fingers, waving papers and faces, the surreptitious passage of Egyptian pound notes, at the epicentre of which would be Twigger frothing with exasperation. Apparently, filling the correct forms in advance would make no difference as to whether our exit was speedy or not, although we were only accompanied once by armed policeman for our protection.

Give or take a final altercation we would head out on the road towards the Bahiriya Oasis, travelling about 200 kilometres before turning off the road over the railway line into the wilderness. The conversation in the cramped land cruiser was lively and provocative. There were only two serviceable seats at the front so those in the back lay on heaps of blankets, boxes, backpacks whilst we discussed everything, quoted bits of poetry, or sang Geordie folk songs. Nick, with his patrician tones and sprinkling pompous assertions around the personal and arcane, was the subject of some teasing as we circled around the path to the happiness and fulfilment of self-discovery. No subject was considered too deep or too trivial for earnest debate. When the 'intellectual bollocky bollocks' as she would call it, got too much for Marie, she would wrap a Bedouin scarf around her face and pretend to sleep.

I had made a playlist and on portable speakers we listened to 'Itsy-bitsy, Teeny-weeny Yellow polka-dot Bikini' in French, Josephine Baker singing 'Breezing Along with the Breeze', Kenny Ball's 'Midnight in Moscow' and 'Besa Me Mucho' by Igor Yusov of the Red Elvises Limpopo Band.

Nick would boom out Shelley in well-hung theatrical vowels:

'I met a traveller from an antique land
Who said: Two vast and trunkless legs of stone
Stand in the desert. Near them, on the sand,
Half sunk, a shattered visage lies, whose frown,
And wrinkled lip, and sneer of cold command,
Tell that its sculptor well those passions read
Which yet survive, stamped on these lifeless things,
The hand that mocked them, and the heart that fed;
And on the pedestal these words appear:
'My name is Ozymandias, king of kings:
Look upon my works, ye Mighty, and despair!'
Nothing beside remains. Round the decay
Of that colossal wreck, boundless and bare
The lone and level sands stretch far away.'

The landscape from the turnoff is at first hard sand covered with little black pebbles; but soon the classic desert opens in front of you and you slip down through a wadi and see the start of the Abu Moharik dune that runs 600 kilometres south east, crossed by centuries-old trading routes, the detritus of which can be discovered in the broken pieces of Roman pottery.

So the desert really is not empty it only appears so. When you look you see the infinite possibilities of supposed emptiness.

Particularly the time we thought we had found the bones of a dinosaur. One of the participants produced a fossilised vertebrate, or at least what appeared to be one, he had found earlier in the day. He had taken it, he said, from a whole line of bones. Robert and I bundled him into the Toyota and quickly retraced our steps since lunchtime. We soon found other long trails of what appeared to be bones up to three metres long, not particularly thick, no more than that of a strong wrist. Also around them remained what appeared to be fossilised fronds. Possibly the bones were also vegetable, but it was more exciting to entertain the possibility that we were looking at the remains of some washed up, ancient crocodiles.

I loved the intense, solid emptiness of the world that surrounds the mighty Abu Maharik dune as much as I loved the chaos of Cairo. In this silent and empty world the evidence of our collective story, is surprisingly easy to find. There are the flat expanses of an ancient lake bed, dotted with weird surreal pillars left by the deposits of springs that had welled up into long-vanished waters, and at the side of which you come across, as if left the day before, the remains of half-finished or forgotten arrowheads, manufactured by Palaeolithic people who sat at the shores of this lake and hunted for fish.

This particular day had been tough for the group. They had been challenged to follow a square-ish course of an average of eighteen kilometres across the dunes, prehistoric lakes and sea beds. The challenge was to navigate by different means, by pacing, using a compass or looking at the shadow lines made by the sun. The challenge was not an end in itself but a chance to create a rare space for reflection and insight. And arriving eventually at the camp was almost always special, for in most cases a sense of adventure was satisfyingly completed. (The adventure emphasised by the fact that they did not know the camp existed.) Usually people lay on the rugs on the sand or in the shade under an awning strung between two 4x4's – a windbreak tied to the back of the third. Saleh made tea. Later he would teach them to make bread.

And now, at the end of the day, they lay exhausted by the heat and the challenge, sleeping, chattering quietly, one sad guy futilely running around holding his mobile phone in the air trying to catch a signal, climbing on to the roof of a vehicle and desperately waving for help.

Going into the desert, I had decided, reveals the soul. Many people were deeply affected by the experience, some of them made anxious by the way the desert invites you to confront yourself.

Often you would see people clearly engaged in the most profound but silent conversation with themselves. Someone told me that it was the first time they had properly met themselves in years.

Others were more disappointing. Some had been hard to like, worse than that, being around them I had found stressful as if they could bleed away my confidence and enthusiasm. They were passive, dully dutiful, cynical, they gave nothing, around them was a cloud of soul-rusting negativity. They seemed to exist as natural microorganisms in the global sea of disaster and futility that ripples around the world: the credit crunch, global warming the loss of value and identity. They were inarticulate about themselves, afraid to explore who they were and who they might be. They were a desert – not the real desert which is simplicity, and clarity but a psychological desert of busyness and cynicism – collectively they were arid. And they looked at the Sahara and saw nothing but sand.

Dazing and gazing down from my vantage point I wondered how we were to be saved? So how do we make our choices well? How do we steer the best path between the twin demands of fitting in and falling out? Balancing the inner voluntary slave and Barbary pirate? Sitting on the edge of the world I really felt I understood the problem but was nowhere near the solution.

I could feel Knulp's attention on me as I speculated. Is it just the fate of some of us to end up emptier than the memory rich desert? In shallows. How do we connect ourselves to the richness and ambiguity of the moment? And stimulated and enriched by this, how do we evolve?

And then I stopped. No, I corrected myself, how do *I* manage this? This whole adventure had been kicked off by my own nostaglia, my own sense of a life not quite lived, my own quest to find a way of steering a more fulfilling path through the possibilities and potential of life. In so many different ways I felt compromised that things were less than they should be. I could and should point out all the times and places that I could accuse myself of procrastination.

And I was of a sudden aware of a lingering, teasing sense of melancholy, the scent of nostalgia. It stayed with me as I wandered down from the dune on which I had been sitting. A little way behind, Knulp followed me as he had, in one form or another, since the start of my journeying.

Saleh and Hamdi were by now absorbed into the act of creating a meal for twenty on a couple of old gas burners and the open fire they had built. Shaking myself into sociable action I banished the ghosts of forgotten promises and roads not taken to the back of my consciousness and laughed, cajoled and prompted the party into a cohesive enough group to be able to eat together, slightly resenting the role of the major-domo.

Saleh's regular miracle occurred again as bowls of lentil soup were passed around, to be followed off by chunks of lamb torn or sliced from the carcass that had been roasting over the fire. Knulp was at my shoulder as a few of us sat around the fire later on as the Bedouin sang and drummed and I accompanied them by beating a rhythm with my outstretched fingers on the back of my old guitar. Saleh sang.

Later that night, people found their own particular spot to slumber and dream, some in little tents erected by the Bedouin, others deep in a new sense of conviviality together under the awning between the vehicles. Twigger as usual had just disappeared into the dark probably to sleep in one of the vehicles; Nick had wandered off to pitch a spot behind a nearby dune from which stentorian snores now kept the desert fox at bay. Marie too was tent bound whilst I, following some primeval instinct, had slung a mat and sleeping bag near the dying embers of the campfire.

I lay on my back and gazed at the frozen rapture of pierced darkness. Being a sad old rocker I plugged in my i-Pod and listened to the melancholy majesty of Dave Gilmour's guitar playing.

Mumbling in the background of my mind was the idée fixe of my day. Nostalgia – what to do about it. And once again I gently mourned the many times I had spurned the potential of the moment, those moments when I had betrayed myself and placed myself in exile from who I should be. How I wondered do I, we, respond better to the unfolding world around us …?

The vast arc of stars and planets and satellites stretched over me, in perfect brightness.

And I felt motionless.

And saw the heavens move. Almost but not quite imperceptibly. Azure flecked with diamonds in apparent transit.

For the first time in my life I was aware of the cosmological progress of time.

And I was still.

At the fulcrum of my existence.

And in a playful reverie I forced my non-scientific brain to wonder what happens to light itself. If we all started in a moment beyond time with a big bang the very instant of which we can still catch at the edge of our technologically enhanced vision, then each moment of time since must continue on if not to infinity, then at least to way past now.

If this could be so, I wondered, lying contentedly in this overwhelming setting, then surely the moments before all the choices we make, are still out there travelling into infinity?

The fiddle bow still hangs motionless in the air.

The narrow boat still floats through a sea of corn.

I was not so deluded I did not think I could catch up with my choices as they hurtled into the blackness, sprinting after to undo them. But every moment I felt was still in a sense available and valuable to me. Nothing was lost. At that moment I felt I could reach every moment of truth, happiness and fulfilment in my life so far.

Silly old fool that I am, the thought made me blissful – close to tears.

The idea that nothing was truly lost or irretrievable dissolved momentarily all self doubt and uncertainty. I became strong. I felt all was to be played for and wisdom to make better choices lay in reflecting upon these moments of travelling light.

Across the dying embers of the fire, in the last whisps of curling smoke, Knulp sat watching me.

'So Knulp', I whispered. 'I am strong but it is the music, memories and the moment that makes me so. How do I stay so? How do I keep on course?'

At first he didn't say anything and supposing he was going to remain silent, I turned my head back to stare at the cosmos and listened to Mr Gilmour. And then I knew he was beside me. I didn't look, scared of fracturing the moment. I sensed him close behind my head and then he whispered in my ear.

'To be really free: be wild, be strong, be experimental, travel with companions and take the first step. These are the rules of the road.'

PART TWO

BE WILD

'Be wild, be strong, be experimental, travel with companions and take the first step. These are the rules of the road.'

Take a chance on the rambling stream
Lose your way, then lose it again,
When a heart hits the road it's born once more
So leave this love
Steve Bonham, The Moon's High Tide

My good friend Lisa, partner of Ben, both experts in bush craft, told me about being out in the woods recently with her ten month old son Finn. He spotted before her a rare red squirrel and watched it without moving or taking his eyes off it for over twenty minutes, never making a noise except for giggling to himself when the squirrel, totally at ease, came within two feet of him.

Finn, I suspect was not thinking: 'where's my camera' or 'pity about the grey ones'. So, he could effortlessly pay attention in a completely wholehearted way. He, like all young children, is born to it; they are naturally wild.

Wildness is a state of mind as well as a state of nature. A state of mind where we can see possibilities and begin to experiment with who we might be. This is not the wildness of anger but as in 'gone wild', unreservedly connected to things that are sensual, sensuous and viscerally present – a state which we often nostalgically seek.

The importance of being immersed in the moment has been an idea and aspiration from time immemorial. Particularly in the east, wise people have sought to free themselves from perceptions formed by our expectation and unconscious emotional judgment aiming to sit in non-judgmental awareness of the immediate moment and observe how things unfold.

To 'Be Wild' seems to capture the elemental and engaged nature of responding to nostalgia. To 'Be Wild' means we are not anchored in the past or the future but in the unfolding possibility of the present. This of course is an elemental survival technique and the need and ability to do it must be etched into our being. It is instinctive to attend to the rustling in the undergrowth, the fleeting shadow as a dark thing crosses the sun, the crack of a twig.

But to 'Be Wild' is about more than survival. It is a route by which we engage with the world, it is part of the essence of who we are. We are born into a world of experience. When we are young there isn't much of a separation between self and the experience, there is a deep absorption between the richness of the moment and our childlike attention – a deep intimate quality.

According to Simon Barnes being 'wild' is about a connection to the environment in which we find ourselves, a connection that comes naturally to us: *'It is my belief that we are all wild; but frequently we seek to express our wildness in strange ways. This is no doubt the result of repression, a result of an unwillingness to incur the censure of society and the strange looks of our neighbours.'*

This state of absorption has been given various names including 'presence' or 'mergence'. Sometimes this state can create the most positive feelings of well-being, sometimes even bliss. It is a state often sought by many through meditation and retreat.

But as with my reflections back in Morocco, I can't help thinking that 'Being Wild' is more than sitting in an uncomfortable position, eyes closed, legs crossed, wobbling on a little stool, but out there, active, sweatily dealing with the world. In so many ways we are what we do, so perhaps it is good to want to do it well with 100% attention.

The psychologist Csikszentmihalyi calls this a state of 'flow'.

When I play my guitar, when I write well, time seems to stand still or slow right down. This is what flow is: it seems attractive, for it positions serenity as active and engaged rather than removed and contemplative. Csikszentmihalyi's research shows in the flow state we feel strong, confident, at the edge of abilities but not beyond them. In 'flow' our perception of time passing is quite different; the moment does not come from anywhere, nor is it going anywhere.

Playfully I wonder if, as we get older, driven to focus on the next thing and the next and the one after that, we spend less and less time focused on the timeless moment of now. This might account for the persistently reported sense that time accelerates as we get older. Perhaps it is the price we pay for ceaseless anticipation that we feel our lives rushing to a close as we chase our own moment of passing, rather than paying attention to each passing moment. In doing so we have lost a relationship with the world which we are born into.

An echo of another memory.

Years ago I can recall regularly walking across the meadow at the bottom of our garden, my first daughter holding my hand. We would climb up the bank of a disused railway line at the far side of the field. Further along was the old station now used by a supplier of agricultural equipment, the curved and sculpted weather boards of the station offices showing remnants of the proud red paint in which they were once resplendent. It was one of Sara's favourite places.

On this particular day we had wandered a little further in the opposite direction where the line bent slightly around a little pond forming in the curve of a stream. It was a warm day and the trackside was full of a profusion of wild flowers: Ox Eye Daisies, Ladies Mantle, Birdsfoot Trefoil. The air was humming with insects and tickled with a breeze as Rosie the dog lay carefully watching us, not trusting me to let the child stray too far. Normally talkative and enquiring, Sara sat in contemplation on the old railway track and gazed in wonder at a single little yellow flower held in her three-year-old hands for a rapturous age. And I had the sudden intense bitter sweet sense that she was in place that I had left forever.

And for me, powerfully and strong, at the earliest point of recall is the cold feel of a Bakelite telephone, the chilly touch of the red quarry tiles of our narrow kitchen, sitting in the garden with the catkins tickling my face, the smell of my brother in his cot, the crackle of the fire in the bedroom fireplace putting a glow on my face even as icy winter fingers touched the back of my neck.

Many of us lose this sensory intimacy as we grow older. We lose the ability to attend wholeheartedly. No longer wild. And this is sad for to 'Be Wild' is to be in a place in which ideas come to us, when things become blindingly clear, when the next step opens up. It is the miracle moment when the future arrives unexpectedly into the present. When the clouds lift and something unexpected becomes obvious.

And the rest is history.

Why do we lose this contact with the world around us, why do we fail to be *wild*?

One distinct evolutionary advantage of we humans is probably that we are pretty good at *anticipation*. We can imagine the future, and we can recall the past or at least our version of it and take lessons from it. These are two immensely powerful tools, through which we can review, learn, plan, imagine, and create. Anticipation is more than a stiffening of the sinews and the summoning of the blood to deal with the imminent, it is also the ability to think well ahead beyond the setting of the next sun.

The giraffe probably does not have a thought process, which allows it to reason: 'Perhaps if I got up early and headed down to the waterhole a little sooner tomorrow I could get a good drink and be back up here amongst the lush foliage before that old lion has opened his eyes and scratched his backside!'

We do. Useful stuff.

Rather critical from a life planning point of view.

From the day a tribal ancestor saw the grey yellow sky, thought of snow and lit a fire, we have survived and thrived because we can learn from the past and anticipate the future. But it has its disadvantages. Living in the past or the future disconnects us from today, the only moment we really have to take action in. It blinds us to the 'possibility' of the present so that we no longer 'see' what is going on. What we see is more determined by what we have seen in the past and what we expect to see in the future.

Psychologists and other scientists have indicated for sometime what we expect to see and what is there often have little relationship to one another. In one famous experiment people are asked to watch a DVD of two teams playing handball and concentrate on particular aspects of the game. Few can recall therefore when a large guy in a gorilla suit walks through the game waving and wanders off again. They refuse to believe such a thing could happen until the DVD is run again and the gorilla pointed out. Seeing may be believing but it's not what's there!

The neuroscientist Antonio Damasio has suggested we have different levels of consciousness: core and extended. Core consciousness is the immediate sense of self we have in interacting with the immediate environment, and awareness of ourselves in a dynamic relationship with our environment. We share this consciousness with most higher mammals: *'Core consciousness is the core self, a transient entity, ceaselessly recreated for each and every object with which the brain interacts'*.

We also have an 'extended consciousness'. This is the consciousness that through memory and learning extends back into the past and on into the anticipated future. This is an important level that we probably only share with chimpanzees and dolphins.

It is our extended consciousness that provides us with our 'autobiographical record', shaping our ongoing conversation with the world through our behaviour in our environment and our 'core consciousness' of it. At best there is an 'intimate relationship' between these two levels of consciousness, but is it unreasonable to speculate that we may lose some of this vital intimacy with the unfolding present as we come, in our busy world, to over-rely on our extended consciousness to deal with an uncertain future?

As well as the developing complexity of our brain processes there is probably another reason why we fail to pay notice fully to the rich paradox of the present: we are taught to be afraid of it. What we consciously pay attention to has already been unconsciously filtered by primitive functions of our brain that 'decide' at an emotional level whether this is a threat or opportunity, certainly in terms of physical wellbeing, but also in terms of our needs for belonging, affection, status, control etc, as the threat of exclusion from the tribe which underpins these can be the biggest threat of all.

In fact I suspect these ancient basic responses have been unconsciously socialized by the tribe which formed us, feeding our perceptions of disasters and rewards. Through this our elders and opinion makers teach us what we to expect to see. From them we learn to curse our neighbours as villains and reprobates, to see heroism in the mundane, to find that which is magical as not. The tribe teaches us to see only the good in some people only the bad and the threatening in others.

So the danger is that we can end up living in a state of endless anticipation of disaster and reward, neurotically judging the situation by our expectations of it and never really seeing the paradox, and potential opportunity, that it contains; or, if we do, it is in such a distorted way that we turn away judging it impossible or irrelevant.

How do we rediscover how to 'Be Wild'? How do we recover this supercharged attention to the present? How do we find ways to reconnect to a more childlike way of being in the world? How do we still our busy minds so that we see?

Rediscovering this childlike gift allows us to be enraptured by the moment. We need to redevelop our quality of attention. I used to play a game with myself sometimes on a train journey. I would choose a fellow passenger and gently observe them, noting to myself features of their face, their clothes, posture. I asked myself to find evidence of who they were and what they were like. Then a couple of hours later I would see what I could recall. Sometimes the intensity of the image lingered on. I can still recall a rather elegant English lady, on an overland section of the London Underground, the sun streaming through the window as we travelled above roof height over the regular semi-detached world of the London petit-bourgeoisie. She was standing up, her arm around one of the train supports holding a book, *The Deptford Trilogy*, if I recall. Her fine features graced by a half smile, as she was lost in the flow of the narrative.

But to 'Be Wild' as we have said does not necessarily mean to be still. It can be about a quality of action as well. Steve Venables, the climber, once told me that you climb around the overhang of rocks above hundreds of metres of nothingness, not by thinking about what happens if you fall or cursing yourself for the sequence of decisions that put you in this position, but by focusing on the rock beneath your fingers, the shape of the face immediately above it and balance of your weight.

I find these days, when I am weary and frustrated by the way my life is going, the trick is not to switch off, retire to the contemplation of a jumble of thoughts and half-baked plans. No, the trick seems to be to switch on; to engage as fully as possible with the world in front of me and discover what it has to offer. So many times I have discovered in the so-doing the wheels of synchronicity turn and a solution to the bigger problems arrives.

So engage. Be immersed. Take a trek.

The lessons of the Moroccan trek have remained and been reinforced many times. When you are travelling at walking pace then two things seem to happen naturally – you engage more with the world directly around you, and then almost miraculously the world becomes simpler, still complex but less *complicated*. I guess many other activities can have this effect, but I believe our nomadic ancestors have gifted us with this particular strategy.

Knulp is wild. He has no future, he is happy to live without one. Nor has he past. He resists being a hostage to either, even when offered the chance to return to his home town to be cared for in his final days. The official past he has, his journey book, full of false work records, exists only to stop him being arrested as a vagrant. His life is a struggle not to have the present squeezed from it. As is ours.

BE STRONG

'Be wild, be strong, be experimental, travel with companions and take the first step. These are the rules of the road.'

It matters not how strait the gate,
How charged with punishments the scroll.
I am the master of my fate:
I am the captain of my soul.

Invictus, William Ernest Henley

There is an amiable little village in Oxfordshire in England close to the River Cherwell, a relative of the Thames. The houses and cottages are often thatched and built of that uniquely warm buttery Cotswold sandstone. Most of the time nothing much happens as the Southern Oxfordshire canal meanders and dallies on its way through, and locals loiter over warm English beer in the Brasenose and the Red Lion. In fact not much has happened here, in Cropedy, since 1644 when Sir William Waller led the parliamentarians into battle against King Charles during the English Civil War and lost.

Apart from one day, every year. First a camper van arrives spluttering a little through the village after a run down the M40; then a Peugeot 307, a Ford and a variety of Toyotas, an old trusty rusty Rover, a middle aged couple on a tandem bicycle grim-lipped with effort, wearing Che Guevara T-shirts, then an embarrassed Mercedes, as coy as a large well-engineered German can be. Soon this trickle of motor locomotion becomes a flood as hundreds then thousands of cars in all states of repair, some pulling caravans, some with little-used tents strapped to the roof, crammed with bearded men, guitar cases, pewter mugs, bored head-phoned children gazing listlessly on England's verdant splendour, big-bosomed women in cheesecloth blouses with grey-blond hair pulled into a pony-tail and everyone else from seventeen to seventy in jeans a size too small.

Each and every year, thousands of people gather in the fields outside the village, to sit in the sun, drink beer, eat a pot pourri of global street food and listen to a folk rock group who only have had one particularly successful album, have never been fashionable and are now in their sixties.

The band is called Fairport Convention and the bass player, Dave Pegg, is someone who was once very kind and supportive of two guys struggling to get somewhere with their music. One of them was me.

Peggy, as he is universally known had a studio in the garden of his large cottage near Banbury, a converted old Baptist chapel. Tim and I had saved enough money from hundreds of gigs in pubs and clubs to record our first album, but not enough to pay for anywhere to stay, typically failing to consider the implications beyond the vague notion we might sleep in Tim's dreadfully old and rusting Renault 12. Peggy took pity on us, fed us, gave us some beers, pointed out where his bathroom was and let us sleep on the studio floor.

I am still in touch with Peggy and a couple of years ago we sat in his house in Banbury having a lunch of smoked salmon bagels and beers. We nattered about old times and the enduring popularity of Cropedy.

'We get full grown adults coming along who were conceived in those fields,' he grinned. He is very modest about the reasons for its continued success. When I asked how it had kept going for over twenty-five years:

'It's about camaraderie and the fact that you're with 15,000 like-minded people, having a peaceful time, some good beer, some good grub and some good music. That's it, that's the gist of what it's all about.'

Too modest I think. I don't want to be fanciful here, but those thousands don't just turn up to drink beer and make babies, or even to listen to the old songs one more time. Amongst the burger and vegetarian wraps, dreadful sunhats and pink skin something very nostalgic is going. Sure, it will be for lost youth and dreams of past times remembered, but also something that is more akin to acknowledgment, recognition, affirmation even. These grey bearded men with shiny heads and battered guitars we recognize, have stayed true to something, stayed strong when others weakened. They kept playing.

'How did this all start?' I asked Peggy.

'It started when I left school and got a proper job, which was in an insurance office in Birmingham. The Royal Exchange, all very nice people, but I knew from the start that it wasn't for me, because by then I'd started playing with all these bands. We were working, we would be gigging three or four nights a week. I was sixteen, seventeen there and we were doing little gigs like youth clubs, and sometimes pubs. It's the proper job syndrome. But I knew that I would play in a band although I didn't realise I'd be doing it for the rest of my life.'

'And how have you kept going?' He paused and thought a while.

'I've got my own little niche in music as I suppose you do in any kind of job that you take on, you find what you're good at, in my case what I thought I was good at was accompanying singer songwriters and playing bass and just being part of the rhythm section and trying to get the song to benefit while I played, not to deter from the song and to kind of add to it and to make it more interesting.

'That's it, sometimes it works, sometimes it doesn't but that's the kind of role of a bass player in this kind of traditional folk music. That was what I felt I was good at, and that's what I enjoy doing the most because I love songs and I love to hear people singing songs and I love backing guitar players. And that for me, is who and what I am.'

What stayed with me afterwards was the simplicity of this as a life plan. So turns a forty year plus career in music, hundreds of recordings, thousands of gigs a million miles on the road: discovering what makes you feel strong, and what gives you pleasure and constantly connecting back to it. Not a drive to be famous, not for adulation, but a simple desire to stay strong, to do what you feel called to do.

Strong?

The word.

What does it make you think of?

Pushing up weights, the smell of cheap perfume; a clenched fist; an iron bar; whiskey; a furious wind; a contender; words; an argument; a tree standing proud?

A tree? That's more like it. A tree, roots deep into the turf; three broad sheltering limbs defying the crash of weather; home to a beady-eyed, red-capped, Green Woodpecker, a yankee squirrel, ants and grubs and what-have-yous. A tree that can reminisce over dry hard summers, incessant rain, long, long summer evenings. A tree; purple at twilight; dressed in icy lace on a pale rice paper morning, dappled olive, sea, emerald, bottle, jade and lime in a glittering sun. In such a tree there is a quality of 'withstanding', there is a sense of virtue, of something passionate in a striving towards the sun.

When Knulp whispered 'Be Strong', this must be what he meant. Not physical power, but a call to root ourselves in those qualities and values that define us. These are our strengths. I have come to believe, they are the essence of who we are. So it would be a sad thing if we were to live a life that did not employ them.

Somewhere along the trail from Derbyshire to Morocco and Hong Kong and beyond I have come to believe that our strengths can be discovered, uncovered, forgotten and recovered but they are of us, more or less immutable, the ore from which we can fashion our unfolding stories.

They are the vocabulary through which our conversation with the world can best take place and are expressed and re-expressed in the unfolding narrative of our lives and in the intense possibilities of the single moment in which we live.

Being strong changes our relationship with the world. It changes the relationship we have from one of power and supplicancy to one that is essentially based on rapport: an interchange with our world based on a sense of worth and understanding .

Is this one of the secrets of Knulp? In the eyes of the people in the lands through which he wanders, he is a failure, a waster, someone who should have achieved something. Yet as he dies, his god tells him he has lived his life as he well as he could have. Is the lesson Knulp teaches us, and in which we can perhaps glimpse our own purpose, not primarily to achieve something grand and lofty but to live as fully as possible in our strengths; regenerating ourselves as we find new ways of expressing them within a changing world. Working with and in our strengths seems at the heart of living a life that doesn't leave us in a more restricted limited world. They are the yarn from which we can weave *and reweave* our lives.

And do we too often lose this sense, this rooted way of being?

On bad days it can seem like the whole world is feeling helpless. The best some can hope to be is 'not too bad' or to be 'getting by'. For the worst it is to feel trapped, without choice, that that which is good or exciting is denied to them. Nostalgia for freedom for some people can be more than a haunting melancholy for a slightly less constraining world but something much darker and unhappier.

Some people feel they have been taken hostage by life.

The psychologist George Kohlreisser is also one of the world's leading hostage negotiators. For him there are striking similarities between the predicaments many people find themselves in in their everyday lives and the situation that a hostage finds themselves in when they have been captured: '*Feeling powerless is one of the first signs of being taken hostage... others can hold people hostage, by situations, or even their own conflicting emotions... Powerlessness poisons the person through feelings of helplessness and entrapment. The poison provokes a continuous negative interpretation of reality.*'

And when this happens, we have handed the power to decide what is happening to us to others. That to me is a killer point. Once we start to feel helpless, the unconscious primitive part of our brain kicks in, and we start to see everything as a threat.

If the essence of who we are is in our strengths, then being distorted or prevented from living through them authentically and well, is not going to be good for us. Such a life would force us off balance, teetering somewhere on the edge, making us sick in body and spirit.

The question is how we free ourselves from the poison of negativity and limiting beliefs about ourselves. It seems to me that some of us spend our lives off balance. In fact a sense of nostalgia for the life we might live and who we might be is perhaps a sense of our feet not standing square on the earth beneath us. Ungrounded our heads are in one place, our hearts in another and perhaps our bodies in yet one more.

It is to our strengths we turn to define and redefine ourselves, they are our reference point in a changing world. They are our hostage negotiators when we find ourselves trapped in an ordinary world. So how do we discover them? Sometimes, as I had recalled in the hotel in London, they arrive in a flash of recognition. Other times we have to explore to find them. This can be difficult. It is The Sinatra Paradox: we can mix up 'do' and 'be' ending with a confusing dobedobedo.

When someone asks us who we are, we often confuse this with what we do. 'Do' is a role or a list of activities 'Be' is something more fundamental, based on our values and passions. I suppose the confusion happens when we define ourselves by our roles in life:

husband, wife, carpenter, dancer, musician rather than the things we bring to them. Strengths determine the way we undertake the roles, the things we do in life. Something that captures the essence of who we are.

So I recall my father sailing his boat. Cap on head, old cigar clamped in his mouth, tiller in hand, seemingly unaware that the boat was at forty-five degrees to the horizon. To say he was a good sailor would be to miss the point – he was someone who could sense in the shudder of the boat the mood of wind, know when it would fluke; he would sense the rain an hour before the clouds gathered, the caprice of the tide. To his core he was a man who could connect to the elements, sense their moods and directions and feel comfortable within them. Towards the end of his life, when he had to step away and stay ashore, the same strengths helped someone who had previously scarcely planted a daffodil, produce the most marvellous, riotous garden. So I guess it is about looking behind what we do, to remember what it is that makes our heart sing.

Being strong is not the same as being famous for something. Nor is it about public approval or ratings or the judgment of others. History is full of those who died unrecognized by their peers, or who were celebrated once and now forgotten.

Being Strong doesn't mean that you have to be especially good at something. It is the thing you do, in the exercise of which you feel energized, it feels simple, obvious, complete, whole. It is when we turn to some inner sense we discover ourselves; when we listen not to the judgement of others but to the quiet clear voice of ourselves. Knulp recalled watching someone from the Salvation Army trying to talk to a crowd in a village who were in a mood to mock.

'They made fun of him and heckled him. Behind him was a young farm hand with a whip. From time to time he snapped it, crack! –to

plague the speaker and everyone laughed. Now the poor fellow didn't get angry, though he wasn't stupid; he struggled against the hubbub with his poor weak voice and smiled where anyone else would have wept or cursed ... there's got to be a great clarity and certainty inside him.'

Knowing our strengths puts us in touch with our genius. This is not about brilliant intelligence but in the old meaning of the word, the spirit that guides you. (The same root as genie and another echo of our cultural next-to worlds.) Genius also came to mean in Roman times the essence of something, its defining qualities and talents. It is our genius that reminds us of the possibilities and next-to worlds around us.

So as the drum kicks in, the fiddle starts to soar, Peggy on the bass, a grin on his face, stoops forward to the microphone to sing the harmony on the chorus, although the songs may and should change, the spirit behind them stays true.

BE EXPERIMENTAL

'Be wild, be strong, be experimental, travel with companions and take the first step. These are the rules of the road.'

Let us say without further ado that life is an affair of flutes. It is overflow that it needs most. He who rests content with barely necessity will be washed away. Life has triumphed on this planet because it has, instead of clinging to necessities, deluged it with overwhelming possibilities so that the failure of one may serve as a bridge for the victory of another.

José Ortega Y Gasset, *The Sportive Origin of the State*

My accidental travels around the globe have taught me many things. Thinking about it, one of the most important is that to feel really free requires an openness to experience and the expectant potential of the world around us. Paddling in the stream of possibility creates a kind of magic in which we can make new sense of who we are and the relationship we have with the world. This means that we have to embrace the confusion and uncertainty that it entails. It is sitting on the bank and watching it flow by that makes us nostalgic.

Living well you see, is a bit of a puzzle. Hanging out with Knulp these few years has really brought it home to me what restless contradictory beasts we are: both pirate and slave with all the muddying and mixed up implications for our personality that it implies. We are driven to fit in and fall out – natural restlessness does daily battle with a strong sense of belonging, conservatism and learned inhibition.

Knulp is a mirror of the paradox in us all: a dissolute and a despiser of drunkenness; promiscuous and passionate by intention but reserved and quaintly formal with several of the willing women he meets; workshy but capable of herculean efforts; dependent on others but determinedly *independent* of them. It's a captivating thought, that we are essentially unpredictable and changeable characters engaged with a world that is shifting, uneven and now and then capricious.

How do we find our way through this? As Van Morrison would say 'No Guru, No Method, No Teacher' is going to solve this for us. The challenge is our own personal life-dilemma for no one else can have the conversation with the world that we must have, our individual vantage point is unique. And though the wisdom of others can be helpful, in the end, 'my life is my own adventure.'

So, I have come to the notion that to evolve and meet the enticing paradox of ourselves and the possibility of the world, we need to be experimental, try things out, be a little dangerous with ourselves. For so it must be in a world which is multi-layered and changing and we with it or against it. And perhaps in doing this we might need to be a little rebellious now and then, not do what's expected, toy with what is prohibited and verboten; surprise, or even shock ourselves and others! And to rebel well, it is helpful if we are not reduced to red-faced self-conscious embarrassment and regret as others tut-tut and stare at us wide-eyed with horrified disbelief as we disrupt the comfortable pattern of their experience of us.

This is a formula for practical evolution – a way of keeping ourselves in constant motion. Experiments are a kind of conversation with the cosmos, in which both parties take part. I try something out, I get a response which can change what I think or how I behave and in doing so I change the cosmos at least at a personal level, just a little.

These are not meandering thoughts of an egomaniac: it's a question of more modest ambition. Simply, it can be trying out unexpected things to see what can be learned. I guess for someone this can be a no holds barred, orgiastic, mescaline-fuelled descent into depravity and a sad conclusion. But it doesn't have to be like that. Being experimental can be another word for being adventurous when 'adventurous' means building some uncertainty and discovery into your travels, whether those travels be metaphorical or otherwise! It is the journey we take to discover more about ourselves, the puzzle of living, and how we best explore our relationship with the world.

A good experiment can mean trying the things that you don't necessarily turn towards – sometimes it is the 'difficult' conversations from which you learn most. One experiment for me was to explore the idea of dancing. It was something that Knulp did well and I don't.

Dancing brings out the shape shifter in us. It reduces strong men with loud voices to the outer regions of the wedding party, lurking, foot-shuffling and eye-avoiding until enough alcohol is consumed; turns the dumpy little girl into a swan; or makes a blonde sylph of loveliness career around like a carthorse on casters.

Dancing was an experiment to find out, rather than an experiment to prove. Although it did prove one thing. I dance like a bear. An enthusiastic bear sometimes. A bear with a sense of the beat. A bear with a certain 'je ne sais quoi'. But a bear none the less. Knew I would, Ursus Major genes.

So why dance? Why, because it seemed something outside of me, something I only dimly understood. People who dance well, dance in another place to other people. You can see in every move and line, the floor does not rise up to meet them causing them to stumble nor does it fall away causing them to sway. Nor do those who dance well gaze into the eyes of another like they are holding onto an axe murderer. Most of all they do not look like they are reciting their thirteen times table in their heads whilst simultaneously recalling the assembly instructions for a particularly fiendish piece of flat pack furniture.

And it is a universal mystery. It turns up in every culture and in almost every social occasion: people dance at births, weddings and deaths. They dance at harvest home, midsummer madness and through winter's brief hours. People dance to tell stories and to forget a troubled day. And they dance to rebel.

Dance can be subversive. Polite society was perturbed by the arrival of the waltz in which a woman and a man could actually touch each other in public in places *other than the hands*, leading an anonymous commentator on etiquette at the time to conclude that she had: '*severe doubts about its morality*' and that it '*ill agrees with the delicacy of women!*'

If the earnest critic had 'severe doubts' about the waltz, she would probably have been profoundly traumatised by the tango. The dance was part-born near the Corrales Viejos, the slaughterhouse district of Buenos Aires and captured the cravings of the poor in the seedy bars, run down dance halls and brothels. It was defiant but melancholy, lost in the swirling nostalgia and longings of immigrants far from home. It was a music where African rhythms met Argentine milonga music, a kind of polka. And the passion was carried not by tender lovers but by the pimp and his prostitute. As Grace Dent wrote in an article in the *Guardian*: '*In Britain, the only time someone touches you like this, they're either your other half, someone you're about to get off with, or you're being sexually molested.*'

So in dance there is the magic of next-to-worlds, through it we can move away from the rules and expectations of the world we are in. Through it we can break free: the couple embrace, the servant defies the master, it opens the door of our cage. We can be wild.

Nearly all the world's dance traditions see the need for dancing to involve both a deep commitment to the steps and a willingness to experiment and improvise. And this experimentation is not usually drawn from some contrived deliberate act of construction but a deep emotional resonance, the echoing possibility of the moment.

It happens in flamenco, in the trance dances of the Bushmen.

What was it that a good dancer has that I so clearly did not? The enigma would not be so resolved by the study but the experience of it. So I went to see Ivan the Slovak's friend Mikaela: a dancer and dance teacher with a passion for salsa.

I had met Mikaela a couple of times before at La Bodequita, a Cuban bar and restaurant with apparently authentic bar furniture from Havana. It always seemed busy with loud salsa music, a meeting place for a younger Czech youth seeking a more energetic rendezvous than the solid beer and sausage ambience of Central Europe on a chilly January night.

Mikaela is vitality and life. She talks with her face, her eyes, her hands, grabbing your arm to emphasise and punctuate, pausing suddenly to think about something connected to another conversation going on somewhere else in her head. The mobile phone is always in reach; she is quite happy to pause the conversation to text a more linguistically gifted friend if she cannot find the English word she is seeking.

We met at a dance studio on a hot day in Prague and were joined by her dance partner Leon an athletic and coordinated looking African.

'Ok Stevey,' she said. 'Let's start with some exercises!'

She turned on a slick Latin beat on her 'Ghetto Blaster', Leon and her gazing into the floor length mirror made bits of their bodies move to the rhythm – one at a time: left hip right hip, left breast, right breast, shoulder, chin.

'This is very important Stevey, you have to be able to move it, feel it, you try.'

The results reduced three people to near hysteria. In an effort to help, Leon and Mikaela would grab hold of bits of me whilst encouraging me to rhythmically move other bits of my body. But how do you persuade your upper rib cage to move without moving your hips or your shoulders? Or your shoulders to go one way whilst your head goes another.

As the afternoon progressed through the basics of Salsa and Samba I was confronted again and again by the presence of a strange new world, not just next-to mine but within it, the language of which was totally alien and awkward.

I never became a dancer, the bear still shuffles, so I share this not as an adventure in dancing but in experimenting. But it was a good experiment. There were moments as I lumbered around to 'Oye Como Va' that I did lose myself in the dance, when it just took over, when I wasn't just dancing it, I was dancing in it! And that was a good place to be. And I saw aspects of who I might be that I had not really considered before. Michaela and Leon have a physical intelligence I can only grasp at. Michaela as a dancer is an actress, she can move, in a quarter beat, from the smouldering aristocratic line of a Spanish flamenco dancer, to the giggling effervescence of the Cuban girl on the street corner who looks sexy and knows it. Leon was smooth, explosive, riffing on the subtleties of rhythm and space. I was not so present: perspiring, demented and blundering for those who remember him, like a slightly hysterical Ted Heath. I realized one huge difference between us was that I was desperately trying to get the salsa, the samba *right*, not make a mistake, whereas Michaela and Leon flirted with the rules, trying to get them, in a particular way, *different*. They were bending the rules, creating new variations, teasing conventions.

And it made me think how we get stuck sometimes being self-conscious when we needed to be self–aware. As I trotted back and forward, carefully stopping to waggle a buttock on the fourth beat of the bar, an incredulous voice in my ear couldn't help but whisper, 'Just what do you think you are doing Rhino-feet!'

Self-conciousness is to attend to the social self, how it looks and will look to others. It is embedded in our extended consciousness; It is checking that what we are doing now fits with the story we tell ourselves about who we are, where we came from and where we are going. Self-awareness is a different thing altogether, it is to be completely absorbed in the moment, in a kind of dialogue with it where the edges of where you stop and the rest begins become blurred. It is like making love: best done with a focus on the matter in hand. Self-consciousness on the other hand can render the most virile of bulls impotent!

I understood as in my terpsichorean reverie that true dancers were eloquent and that eloquence was based upon a highly aware but unselfconscious inhabitation of the body that carries us. Is not this the state of mind of adventurousness and experiment; absorption and a willingness to let go, of expectations, the internalised voice saying 'go back'?

Maybe self-consciousness is a kind of learned social control, a kind of internalised 'others'-consciousness' asking us: 'What would other people think? What would other people say? Will I look how I am supposed to look?' No wonder the wallflowers cling to the walls at weddings. And I think self-consciousness, this voice in the ear saying uh-uh and no-no, must be closely associated with feeling inhibited, and the origin of nostalgia.

Self-consciousness is a kind a self-imposed limitation on who we might be and is worthy of rebelling against. Seeing ourselves and the world in new and novel ways is the best way of meeting a fundamental requirement to be rebellious. In fact being experimental is an essentially revolutionary act requiring you to want to question and undermine beliefs, assumptions and cherished 'truths'. Without it we will stagnate.

Perhaps, therefore, we need to let go a little more of the need to 'fit in' in consistent and dutiful ways for we are born to be restless experimenters seeking to reconcile conflicting aspects of our character. Sometimes we will do this well, but the resolution is necessarily only temporary and we must continue to evolve and seek new solutions. Not to do so is to deny part of who we are.

One way to start to move on from this and also the tyranny of self-consciousness is to realise how arbitrary are so many of the things we feel we couldn't, or shouldn't do. There is a rather wonderful book by Taras Grescoe called *The Devil's Picnic*. It recounts a year he spent travelling the world consuming food and drink banned in various countries. This included: Marks and Spencer's poppyseed crackers and chewing gum in Singapore; Epoisse French cheese in New York; and absinthe in Switzerland, and a long search in Spain to consume threatened-with-a-European-ban bulls' testicles.

The core message of the book is that from the beginning of organised society those with the power to shape what is deemed acceptable have actively sought to keep the rest of us in check. In fact, what is often addressed to us in terms of what is good for *us* is just a wind up. Some days I think the most insidious and elusive control is the social value that regards dependability and predictability as positive and changeability and unpredictability as necessarily negative and anti-social.

I have come to see it is how we respond to this that matters. Will we be taken hostage by it? The temptation is to compromise, to reconcile as in to make friendly, to nearly do... But I think now to be really alive we should not compromise if compromise means such surrender. In some part of our lives we must be wholly a revolutionary if we are to be true, if we are to be who we really want to be rather than settling for who we nearly want to be.

But it is not only ourselves but the tribes we live in that need to learn to evolve, to keep pace with the changing circumstances in which we exist. We need to allow rebellious ideas from which we can adapt and change. This gives our tribes a rather uneasy relationship with rebelliousness: providing as it does, the potential seeds of our destruction and the essentials for our renewal. Individually, we are both the defenders on the ramparts and the barbarians at the gates of the tribes to which we belong.

A great example of this need for orthodoxy and rebellion is the story of the painter Manet. In the middle of the nineteenth century he started to paint in a way that the upset the conventions of socially acceptable 'good art'. In his pictures, real women stare back at you from boldly painted canvases of apparently crude brushstrokes, whereas his more conservative contemporaries executed with microscopic attention to detail, enraptured and rather portly nymphs floating on clouds above an Arcadian temple. In places he appears to have missed bits and it seems patches of canvas poke through. For several years he was scorned by the conservative elite of Paris, his paintings actively prohibited by civilised opinion from being hung on the walls of the Salons. But then people grew tired of the old tasteful art, and looked for something more vibrant and challenging and as Manet shaped and influenced other painters with similar sensibilities, he ended up being the leader of the new conservative orthodoxy. Art like our tribes and ourselves evolves on the axis of stability and change.

So perhaps we should recognize that we are all naturally inconsistent and to be so is not the terrible social misdemeanor that it might appear. Actually it may be simply to recognise the reality that the vast majority of people are often inconsistent although they may develop creative skills to appear otherwise.

Mike Apter is in one of the world's most interesting psychologists. Originally from Bristol he now lives with his wife Mitzi down on the Bayou in Louisiana. In a series of clever experiments in the 1970's he showed how to be human is to be naturally inconsistent to the extent that we can, on different occasions see the same thing in quite different ways. e.g. the same crying child can invoke reactions of compassion, dutiful concern or frustration, irritation, etc.

Or to take another example. Sitting in the armchair reading a cheap novel can be one of life's little pleasures except when you suddenly feel frustrated with yourself and feel you should be doing something worthwhile.

These situations represent for Mike Apter 'reversals' between different motivational states, different ways of seeing, in fact of being, in the world. And these different motivational states act like lenses in which different aspects of a situation will be seen as important and different emotions evoked. Mike Apter proposes that we are essentially paradoxical: on the one hand, that we are motivated to be purposeful or future-oriented; and on the other that we want to live and play in the moment; that we seek sometimes to deal with each other in terms of power and status but on other occasions in terms of affection and care; that we seek to see the world sometimes in terms of how it impacts upon others and other times how it impacts upon us. Perhaps the motivational paradox most pertinent to a little nostalgia for freedom that Mike Apter highlights are the conflicting desires to conform and break free. At one moment we can feel warm and safe wrapped in the bosom of our family or community or tribe then in another constricted, suffocated, trapped and needing to escape.

People I know and respect have called Mike's research 'courageous' and 'liberating', for it recognizes our own paradoxical nature and rids us from the socially imposed tyranny of being tirelessly consistent. In the end, the beauty of an experiment is that it is about finding out about, not necessarily committing to, a course action. If you can think about something, sense its potential then it is worth an adventure – where the adventurous journey is a literal or metaphorical call for experiment, exploration and discovery. It is where we find the wanderer within – our inner Knulp.

What makes an adventure? It isn't just the place. If you can get tour guides to take you up Everest, and companies that can take you almost anywhere with a clear itinerary and a tight schedule, then an adventure is not so much about where you go but how you get there. It's a subjective thing. Adventurous journeys are ambiguous, you don't know each night where you will stop; you can't guarantee to get to your destination; but most of all there has to be a challenge that you don't have complete confidence you can meet. It is under these conditions you learn so much more about yourself, discovering and re-discovering aspects of who you are that open up new possibilities or allow you to engage with present circumstances in different ways.

I had always thought that 'adventures' were something other younger, fitter, braver people did. People who thrash themselves into shape in early morning gyms, have learnt to tie complicated knots and who go for weeks only eating witchetty grubs. But then, a few years ago, my father, a very competent sailor, who had always planned to sail the Atlantic when he retired, died. One of the impacts upon me, was an overwhelming need to re-order my life and put the outdoors somewhere into it. So I looked for adventures, little adventures that I could manage. The trick was not see myself in competition with super athletes but, with due care and preparation, find something that challenged me.

I learned to choose adventures, with respect to myself and my abilities but not being afraid to explore what is possible. The trek though the Atlas Mountains was tough-ish but took no special skills, the desert is hot and again tough, but flat. Sometimes it's all about self-talk.

Robert Twigger and I had talked about this on our several trips into the Sahara. He sees the search for adventure as vital to the successful realisation of who we are and champions small scale, low budget, 'd.i.y.' expeditions. Although he has caught the world's longest snake; was the first person to cross Western Canada in a birch bark canoe since 1793; and has hunted for lost oases in the Sahara and bona-fide zombies in Haiti (and found them), he is keen that adventures are personal.

Sitting under an unbelievable heaven in the Sahara one night, we had talked about the 'unknown and the undiscovered'.

'There's plenty of adventures to be had and exploring is a great way of having them,' he went on. 'It depends how you look at it. Exploring is as much about recording a place with new eyes as anything else. Sometimes retracing another explorer's steps can be so illuminating. When I crossed Canada in the canoe, we got to one point described in the 1793 expedition – a log jam – where absolutely nothing had changed in 200 years!

'There are so many possibilities – and you just never know what you will find and where it will take you.'

A perfect example of a 'd.i.y' adventure is told by Sandy McKinnon in his book *The Unlikely Voyage of Jack de Crow*. An Australian teaching in an English public school, he decided to leave at the end of the summer term. Bidding adieu he left not in a car or taxi or train but in a rather decrepit Mirror dinghy. He intended to sail through English canals and rivers *'just to see where I got to – Gloucester near the mouth of the Severn, I thought'*. But then one thing led to another and despite some rather dodgy map reading and planning and a variety of water borne misadventures, he ended up having sailed around the English coast from London and across the Channel arriving a year later, having covered 4,900 kilometres, by the Black Sea in Rumania. (A Mirror dinghy is totally open and just over three metres long!)

It's not that we should all attempt something as extreme as this, but the spirit of Jack de Crow captures something about an adventurous experiment: we don't want to care too much where we sleep each night, it shouldn't be overplanned; it is about discovery and surprise not premeditated objectives; we need to travel light prepared to gather useful things on the way. And we need to be prepared to be disconcerted.

Being experimental may mean we have to accept that at some moments we seem to have become disconnected from who we were but have not yet grasped where we are going. I remember a year ago when computers first started doing more interesting things than mental arithmetic and electronic table tennis, there was a programme that could stage by stage change one image into another. Say a duck into a swan. In this pictorial journey, the duck started to lose its duckness altered by yet unrecognizable qualities of swanness until there was a point of total confusion. It is a natural moment of change, in which it is probably best to expect, accept and move on.

Like the other Rules of the Road, being experimental is as much a state of mind as anything else. Perhaps the image of dancing is potent: the idea that the freedom to evolve requires knowing the steps and patterns of belonging with the self-awareness and lack of inhibition to try things out safely within the next-to world of the dance.

In Ireland in the old days on warm sunny evenings at the cross roads outside of country villages, young men and women would meet to sing and dance with each other, free from the stern official face of the priest, parent and policeman. It was a chance to flirt, explore, charm, dare and be dared. To taste a more adventurous life, a more audacious life.

This practice was banned by law with the Public Dance Halls Act in 1935.

TRAVEL WITH COMPANIONS

*'Be wild, be strong, be experimental, travel with companions
and take the first step. These are the rules of the road.'*

*Jenny, I said, nothing could be so wrong,
As to climb down this hill, and head home again,
Was it really there, could you hear it breathing,
Across the holy water, a glimpse of Avalon*
Steve Bonham, Looking Back on England

What have we lost as we play with our increasingly shiny new
toys, and scheme our schemes on silver aeroplanes in a world
that hums with electronic connection, when for the price of a
dollar anyone can know anything about anyone? What have we
lost? We have, I am told, lost our privacy, our individualism: Big
Brother and his nasty little niece Miss Celebrity Culture is
everywhere.

But it is the oddest thing – with everything from the size of our
underwear to the probable date of our death out there to be known
by the curious and mildly insane – with no barriers to access, we
are lonely. When we chat to friends we have known all our lives via
the internet we are more available than we could ever have been.
And yet many of us feel disconnected. We live in communities
where our neighbours are often strangers to us. In towns that are
not where we were born.

So what have we lost?

A sense of belonging.

Of being born into a tribe.

Is this why one of the popular websites is about helping people trace their ancestors?

I wonder if one of the qualities experienced by people who live in more traditional communities is that a richer array of relationships is available. Sometimes it seems in the age of the 'nuclear and disintegrating family', relationships with relatives are more distant, less involving, same sex friendship groups are weaker more superficial, we have lost a sense of interdependency.

Certainly the globalised society has broken many of the bonds of our tribal heritage. In some ways this may be no bad thing. For every tribe there is a population not in it, people who are 'not us' and therefore we may treat as objects. But in fracturing these bonds many of us feel disconnected. It seems for many people their destiny is to end up somewhere adrift.

Now people have always moved, in fact it is part of our restless instinct to do so. But for the vast majority, this was a mass movement in which a 'sub tribe' regenerated itself in a strange land. The Irish in Boston; Chinese, and Jewish communities all over the world; my dear friend Charlie, marching up and down in full woollen Scots regalia blowing on bagpipes under the pitiless sun of Queensland, Australia. Even today, the somewhat desperate cliques of British expats clinging together in exotic places to take tea and play golf.

What is different I believe is, as the merciless global mixing bowl goes about its business more and more people are not sure of their tribe or the community they belong to, and as a result, hang on to some symbolic remnant – the sports team of another nation – like a vestigial tail, a reminder more of something lost than something current and shaping.

This need to belong to a tribe and define our lives in relation to it is even found in the global digital world of the internet. Up in cyberspace tribal connections are built which are defined by shared vocabulary and develop their own rituals and protocols with the capability of excluding the outsider. Even anarchists, those who most reject the ties of belonging, are drawn to acknowledge their tribalism. The anarchist writer Hakim Bey, has written about the ability of cyberspace to allow the creation of Temporary Autonomous Zones, short lived communities which the CIA and other special forces of decadent capitalism cannot immediately shut down.

And perhaps our current obsession with social media such as Facebook and Twitter is simply a reflection of a deep need within us to connect and share. To share: opinions, feelings, objects, thoughts. Evolutionary Psychologists such as Robin Dunbar have argued that language itself is less about functional problem solving and more about building communities through chatter and gossip, enabling a sense of cohesion and identity to develop. In fact Robin Dunbar argues that it was the connecting /reassuring function of language that enabled human groups to evolve to 150 person tribes from the much smaller groupings of other primates which are held together by *physical* grooming, a much more time consuming activity. It is a rather wonderful thing to think of, that the vast majority of our on and off line chatter is basically the metaphorical search for bugs, twigs and mucky skin that reassures and enables us all.

I believe it is our tribal ancestry which necessarily draws us to function best in groups of people we trust and feel connection with. The word that describes this best for me is 'companionship'. The root of the word comes from the latin *com* meaning 'with' and *panis* meaning 'bread'; simply those we share bread with, with all the mutuality and trust that that implies. And yet it seems to me, highlighted by our compulsive search of the wireless desert, we live increasingly in societies in which companionship is under pressure. Is it because we have been disconnected from our tribal nature? And through this, the way we relate to others seems to have shifted from a deep awareness of the collective whole to something that is brittle and transient.

Of the many things the search for nostalgia helped me see, one of the things that has haunted and intrigued me most was the realization that companionship was at the heart of our human experience. That it was more than a soothing analgesic to the vicissitudes of our individual journeys. Over the time that followed since then I have come to see that it is both the reward for our fitting in and the means to sustain our adventurousness, our rebellious, audacious journey.

Companions as I realized back in Hong Kong are part of the warp and weft of almost every culture and celebrated in its stories and tales, from the *Band of Brothers, Secrets of the Ya Ya Sisterhood, Snow White and the Seven Dwarfs* etc. In them all is woven a cloak which can keep out the bitterest blast and shade us from the most relentless glare. Every guru from Jesus, Buddha to Freud and Elvis was sustained and enabled by the love and friendship of those around them. Though in all they must face a defining moment on their own, it is through their friends and companions they have been sustained and nurtured for this moment.

And every Don Quixote has a Sancho Panzo.

And so it is with us, to grow and flourish the conversations and attention from others in whom we feel we have trust, rapport and a sense of shared identity, will really matter. Instinctively, we understand the basic human need to be heard. If we are not heard we don't feel whole. But it is more than that, it is through conversations that most times we think and decide. It is in the ebb and flow of the dialogue of the common man and woman that ideas are born and nurtured, dreams are shaped into reality, a wild notion becomes a life changing opportunity.

And I believe this has always been the way; since the beginning, since the first non-verbal moment when we looked at each other and recognized our common cause.

Some while after the Hong Kong trip I found myself sitting under a big African night sky around a campfire in Northern Namibia spending some time with the bushmen of the Ju/'Hoansi San, tribe. I was with Werner Peiffer a gentle bearded German Namibian.

'In the old days,' he said, staring into the fire as if he could see in it back to the days before the bushmen were the victims of generations of genocidal attacks and their culture despised, fractured and almost destroyed. 'In the old days, one person trying to dominate a group such as this was really resisted. Anyone who did try to dominate and dictate what was said, was first challenged, secondly ignored or ostracised, and thirdly, in the *old* days, if someone simply persisted in being domineering, killed!'

The haunting image I have is of people around the campfire not just sharing the stories that tell them who they are, what they should believe and how things should happen but also planning, problem solving, decision making, making sense of the world together. Thinking together and understanding together. In the flickering firelight, voices from faces shining with reflected light and etched in shadows, offer ideas, views, bits of history which meet in the smoke to become a whole. Through this the path of the antelope, the source of fresh water or a whole cosmology, a richer picture of how the universe is, may be conjured.

Often in these conversations there is a pause after one person has spoken. A pause not to think of an argument against but to consider carefully what has just been said. And implicitly this act of conversation is also an act of communion.

Communion in being part of something bigger than yourself.

Communion in being in an intimate relationship with those around you.

If 'Being Wild' implies an intimacy with the animate and inanimate environment, a deep rapport with the rock, the soil, the scudding cloud, the bird on the branch of the tree; then we also have within us the need and ability to be intimately connected with other people. This is not just the physical intimacy of lovers or a parent and a child, but an emotional and spiritual identification with another. It's a surprisingly practical quality of being human.

It's like playing music together. Playing around the clubs with my old chum Tim we would have a repertoire of over a hundred songs and tunes. Rarely did we ever bother with a 'set list' or running order, or if we did we would soon ignore it. You see, we just knew what to play next based upon an inarticulate but powerful sense of where we were and where the audience was. Often we didn't tell each other or the audience what we would play next we just started: on time, together. Sometimes half way through a tune Tim would change rhythm, or tempo and I would just know. All of this was a rough and crude version of what any half decent jazz band can do. Or any great football team. Or theatre company. Or family. It is how Bushmen hunt, how they survive in a difficult and extreme environment, or as Werner says, how they decide.

Without this collective inner harmony, it seems to me that groups of people can only at best function in a self-conscious, rather forced and rather clunky way. Which I suspect is how many of us do, much of the time.

Intimacy goes way beyond 'belonging', it is tapping into the essence of who we are, and may be that is why it can become a rare and vulnerable thing. But it is the well-spring from which companionship draws life. What hurts one of us, hurts all of us. And this seems a natural not learned thing. Neuroscientists, have proposed the existence of 'mirror neurons' in the brain that 'fire' when something is observed happening to someone else. So we see someone bang his or her head and say 'ouch' or one gets too close to the fire and we wince. And the closer we are to the person we are observing the stronger the effect is. This reaction is unconsciously prompted.

So from the bushmen tracking in the first light of dawn, the oryx, the kudu and the porcupine through the millennia, this intimate shared consciousness has woven people together, has continued to shape who we are: collaborative, connected, concerned. A large part of us is essentially collaborative, as more and more research in evolutionary psychology seems to reveal. This collaboration provides us with a set of social behaviours which can easily be overlooked in the picture of the individual free-agent acting only out of self-interest. We sometimes underestimate our capacity for self-sacrifice, working for the greater good and the simple love of working with our fellows.

In my lifetime I have seen groups of people face tear gas, beatings and bullets from Rumania to Cairo and Damascus in the hope of something better for everyone. Collaboration is a clear and present feature of Confucian thinking but is also a powerful if less celebrated feature of western behaviour. All this must be rooted in our ancestry, in the stalking of the game and the irrigation of the fields we have evolved to look after each other. Without it we could not have survived.

This is a fantastic ability through which we can build on the wisdom of others. And in such conversations we, without awareness, tap into the wisdom and insight of our ancestors. The freedom to evolve, to renew ourselves or even to survive may be a hard one, even an impossible one unless we travel with companions. Knulp depended time and again on his friends to sustain him in the life he had chosen, friends who nourished and encouraged him even though they were perplexed and confused about the choices he had made.

The alchemy we need in our search for freedom.

The question is, who do we identify with and feel we belong to? Or would it be better to say, who should we focus on belonging *with*? As Nick 'the Desert' noted, many of our friends do not wish to come with us on our journey. We can love and respect them for this but we must not let them tie us to living in the past. We can keep and cherish them but also seek companions who can help us evolve.

I have been lucky in my life with some of my friends. And now I think about what the quality of those relationships is and has been. Yes there is rapport, that wonderful, special instinctive understanding between people who are not kith or kin but whose lives have become enmeshed through shared stories and a kind of sublime chemistry. Yes there is rapport but there is also synergy. The best companions are distinguished by important differences and who, arising from these differences, are not afraid to confront, clash and conflict with another. Those I cherish do not seek to control me but to challenge my path so that I evolve well. This is a tough love that is distinguished by its rarity and its bravery. It is a special friend who will risk the regard of another for their love for them.

The best of companions are not wholly like us, they may only travel with us part of the way, they may be on parallel journeys themselves and we should give them the space to be so. I have been in the desert with companions and I have been in the desert with accidental fellow travellers. With the former I emerged encouraged and renewed, with the latter I merely survived.

TAKE THE FIRST STEP

'Be wild, be strong, be experimental, travel with companions and take the first step. These are the rules of the road.'

... Start close in,
don't take the second step
or the third,
start with the first
thing
close in,
the step
you don't want to take

David Whyte, *Start In Close*

That is it, isn't it? We may feel the call to adventure, be in touch with the possibility of our world, see how we might evolve. We know what we want but in front of us is a yawning chasm over which we must take the first step.

This is the moment of truth, the choice between nostalgia and freedom. We can see, almost touch, our next-to-world. And we find ourselves caught in a crisis of indecision. Like the diver on the edge of the high board looking down at the extent of the plunge he is about to take, pausing for a few seconds, minutes, hours, weeks, months, years. A life time. Or he, and we, slink away, frustrated even angry with ourselves. 'Next time', we promise ourselves. 'Next time'.

I guess in the end it's almost like stage fright. That moment just before you go on as you hear the murmur of the audience and you desperately try to hang on to your opening line as you tumble from looking outwards through your own eyes to suddenly seeing yourself through every critical, prejudiced, malevolent, superior, more worthy, pair of eyes in the audience.

And you look small and unprepared and so desperately out of place.

And in that moment when you judge yourself so harshly then you are frozen fearful and ready for flight.

What has happened? What has got to happen to take that step, the step into the now of rebellion and evolution? Why do we totter on the tipping point and how do we let go of the past and embrace the future? Or as Joseph Campbell put it: '*If a person has a sense of the call, but remains in the society because it is safe and secure, then life dries up*'.

It was interesting when I asked some of my friends what the issue around taking the first step was. Those who, it could be argued, had fallen further out of the mainstream; writers, explorers were simple and brutal about this hesitation calling it a 'laziness' or a 'lack of perspective', or wrote handy tips on how to get over it. For others, those who might feel 'voluntary slavery' was a state they understood, the question was more troubling, as if asking it was in itself vaguely threatening: 'uncomfortable'. It was something you ended up 'turning 360 degrees around.'

Perhaps part of taking the first step is to really understand what is happening. We should perhaps not be surprised that we might hesitate, for in this moment of truth we are about to destroy a key part of our identity, part of who we have been. We are about to distance ourselves from the tribe, step into being someone else. For this we feel we may be ridiculed, ostracised, accused of betrayal. We may be 'getting above ourselves', 'letting people down', 'being ridiculous'. 'Who do you think you are?' we hear others taunt. It may well be that people don't or won't say these things, but we believe they might think them. Or even more insidiously we say it to ourselves.

And on top this fear of rejection, humiliation and hurt is fearing the loss of our companionship, love of belonging, the sweet ties that bind. Nick 'the Desert' thought that 'We may not just lose a bit of the past but everyone who loves us in the present. For they have an investment in keeping us the same. They don't want us to change. So if we want to transform our life by even taking one small step the last people we should tell are those who love us.'

Too strong a claim?

Surely not all our first steps are so dramatic? Perhaps not all. I guess there are standing-still first steps in which we just do the same thing differently and there are real first steps in which the act of taking changes us.

I had an old psychology lecturer at University. He had learned, and spoke, dozens of languages – taking up a new one each year. Except some languages, he once modestly told me, weren't really new ones, they were just versions of old ones he had already learned albeit with new words. He would recognize as real first steps, new languages that gave new insights into the structure of thought, or the culture of the people who created it, or a new way of looking or being in the world.

Real first steps are when we pull the sword from the stone and a fresh story takes over our lives. A step that will change how we are seen, or how we see ourselves. It could be almost anything that is surprising, bold and unexpected. It doesn't have to be big but in some subtle or not so subtle way we sense it will change our relationship with the world and with ourselves. Intuitively we understand something profound is at stake.

Over the years through my adventures I have been the witness or even a participant in activities in which someone takes a critical step, one they have shied away from perhaps on several occasions. It might be an abseil, tipping over a cliff on a length of rope and walking down at right angles to the rock face. It might performing to a small audience a song you have learned. It might be finally saying what you really think.

In every case, in taking that step people almost in a daze afterwards, say they feel changed, that from now on things will look differently to them. Some of the greatest joy I have taken from my work has been to feel I have been a little catalyst in such moments.

The psychologists Keegan and Lahey in a book called *Immunity to Change*, reflect upon how we often undermine a real determination to change by having a 'competing commitment', often obscure or hidden to us which undermines this intention. This hidden commitment is protecting us from some fear or anxiety. And what prompts this fear is a big assumption about how the world works. They describe the effect of this on our ability to take that step as like driving with your foot down and the brakes on!

Importantly this competing commitment is a reasonable response to paradoxical demands. Perhaps in this case it is between the pleasures of voluntary slavery and the freedom to evolve. Behind this fear of taking the first step is therefore probably a big assumption that if I leave who I am, *I will be unloved*. Surely this is the big black shadow that lurks at the edge of our attention, the eyes watching us in the undergrowth, the warning growl at the edge of darkness? But it is an assumption! Not a fact! I wonder if we don't have a tendency to universalize and make catastrophic our fears? Don't we assume that something will inevitably happen? And that when it does the result will be undoubtedly disastrous?

We should see this assumption for what it is – the primeval socialization of the tribe playing itself out in our feelings about who we are and who we might be. Our well-meant unconscious fear response, designed to stop us being eaten has been hijacked to make sure we don't stray towards a next-to world. And who has planted these deep triggers: our parents, teachers, elders, distant voices from our childhood and further?

To avoid the stage fright that immobilises us, it is these voices we

185

must overcome, so that we can look outwards once more through our own eyes, standing on the solid ground of our strengths running through the evidence of our rehearsal; not judging what is about to happen, not trying to claim the future when we belong in the present. So that we can focus on our performance, on doing it as well as we possibly can, enjoying the technicalities, the deployment of skill and sense of performance.

So how might we take the first step? The first four rules of the road support us. When we are on the solid ground of our strengths; when we are wild enough to see the possibility around us; when we are willing to experiment with who we are; and when we have true soul mates who encourage us to go forward not hold us back lest we threaten their world.

And then perhaps the solution is that proposed by 'Brahim the Berber. Take shorter steps but don't stop.

Take the step you can manage, remember the physics; stride length times height can quickly make the effort exhausting.

Take the step towards what you intuitively know is the right direction. Don't get involved in battles in your head between the voice of the tribe and the voice of freedom.

Take a smaller step. Don't imagine the first step is the whole journey. Don't deny yourself the pleasure of the journey of getting there by imagining it can be done in one bound. Enjoy the feeling of momentum building and a new story taking shape. A new story which as you sit in the late evening by a crackling fire, as a cold wind rattles and mutters outside the door, as the clock ticks towards midnight, you are proud to tell.

Sometimes just stand still and strong and wild and let the future come to you.

AN ENDING

The snow hung like soggy white woollen hats on the branches of the pine trees. Every so often a branch would dip gracefully and the snow would slip protesting to the ground with a baritone 'plomp'. Elsewhere in the forest, at the pace of a chilly sloth, would come and answering 'per-lomp'. Above, the arched trees were like a great leaking roof through which glanced filaments of light, turning momentarily to a fierce beam, as a slight breath of wind changed the alignment of the upmost branches.

I lay head to head with Knulp who was wheezing slightly.

'You Ok Knulp?' I asked

' I am,' he answered quietly.

We lay in companionable silence listening to the forest.

'Thank you Knulp,' I said.

'For what?'

'For making me think, for sharing my restlessness.'

In the undergrowth a weasely creature moved, an eye blinked,

'For being a go-between.'

Knulp was quiet so I prattled on.

'The rules of the road, they're not easy are they? They ask a lot of us. They feel ... don't know, intimidating, I guess.'

The wheezing stopped.

I closed my eyes. The air felt warmer. There was a faint scent of Spring.

Grateful acknowledgement is made to the authors of works quoted in this book. Every effort has been made to contact copyright holders where permission is required.

'Leaves' by Derek Mahon from New Collected Poems (2011) by kind permission of the author and The Gallery Press www.gallerypress.com.

'Barges' by Ralph McTell published by Onward Music Limited.

History as a System, and Other Essays Towards a Philosophy of History by José Ortega Y Gasset copyright 1941 © 1961 by W.W Norton& Co Inc., New York.

London River by H.M. Tomlinson originally published Alfred A Knopf, Inc. 1921, reprinted by Kessinger Publishing

'The Glory' by Edward Thomas from Collected Poems (2004) Faber & Faber

Knulp by Hermann Hesse. Translation © Farrar Straus Giroux Inc 1971. First published in Great Britain by Jonathan Cape 1972

Travels with a Tangerine by Tim Mackintosh-Smith, Copyright © Tim Mackintosh-Smith 2001. First published 2001 by John Murray (Publishers) Ltd, London.

In Morocco by Edith Wharton. First published in the UK in 1920 by Jonathan Cape Ltd.

Wild Ceylon by R.S. Spittel. General Publishers, Colombo, 1945.

'Nomad Invasions' by Bruce Chatwin. Reprinted in What Am I Doing Here? Copyright © the Estate of Bruce Chatwin, 1989. First published in Great Britain by Jonathan Cape Ltd, 1989.

The Sea and the Jungle by H.M. Tomlinson. Originally published in 1912. Reprinted in Great Britain by Duckworth, London: 1930.

Mister Dog by Margaret Wise Brown. Originally published in 1952 by Simon & Schuster, Inc. Copyright © 1952, renewed 1980 by Random House, Inc., New York.

'Bump' by Spike Milligan. Published in The Little Pot Boiler by Dobson Books, Ltd, December 1963

THE MOON'S HIGH TIDE
A JOURNEY THROUGH LOST SUMMERS

Take 11 acoustic songs by Steve Bonham recorded in Co. Mayo with old friends and some of the best of Irish musicians, and the result is A Journey Through Lost Summers.

Songs like an old cat stretching in the sun, songs of a dusty road, songs of place, people and memory. Songs of wry regret and songs of stubborn joy.

Songs about what once was and will ever be. . .

Find out more at:
www.stevebonham.net